# SEIZE THE CORE OF THE TOEIC® TEST

Masako Yasumaru
Noriko Sunagawa
Reiko Akiyoshi
Yasushi Totoki
Akiko Watanabe
Andrew Zitzmann

**KINSEIDO**

**Kinseido Publishing Co., Ltd.**
3-21 Kanda Jimbo-cho, Chiyoda-ku,
Tokyo 101-0051, Japan

Copyright © 2015 by Masako Yasumaru
                    Noriko Sunagawa
                    Reiko Akiyoshi
                    Yasushi Totoki
                    Akiko Watanabe
                    Andrew Zitzmann

*All rights reserved. No part of this publication may be reproduced, stored in a retrieval system, or transmitted, in any form or by any means, electronic, mechanical, photocopying, recording or otherwise, without the prior permission of the publisher.*

First published 2015 by Kinseido Publishing Co., Ltd.

Design     Shigoka Co., Ltd.

🎧 音声ファイル無料ダウンロード

http://www.kinsei-do.co.jp/download/4004

この教科書で 🎧 DL 00 の表示がある箇所の音声は、上記 URL または QR コードにて無料でダウンロードできます。自習用音声としてご活用ください。

▶ PC からのダウンロードをお勧めします。スマートフォンなどでダウンロードされる場合は、ダウンロード前に「解凍アプリ」をインストールしてください。
▶ URL は、検索ボックスではなくアドレスバー（URL 表示覧）に入力してください。
▶ お使いのネットワーク環境によっては、ダウンロードできない場合があります。

◉ CD 00　左記の表示がある箇所の音声は、教室用 CD（Class Audio CD）に収録されています。

# 本テキストの特徴とその使い方

　グローバル人材の育成と確保が求められる中で、ますます多くの企業が、英語力を測る目安や採用・昇進の判断材料として TOEIC を利用しています。また近年では、大学においても TOEIC のスコアをレベル判定や成績評価に用いたり、大学院の進学要件としたり、合否判定の優遇措置としたりするケースも増えてきています。

　このように TOEIC の需要が高まる中、高いスコアを取得するためにはどうすればよいのでしょうか。地道な努力を重ねることが必要なのは言うまでもありませんが、それに加えて、全体の構成・分量・時間配分などを把握し、ビジネス関連の語彙や表現、そして TOEIC のテスト形式そのものに慣れることも重要です。しかしながら、ただひたすら問題を解いて頻出の出題パターンと自分の弱点を攻略するというのは、なかなか大変な作業です。

　そこで、TOEIC を熟知した著者陣による問題の徹底分析の結果に基づいて作成された「超実践 TOEIC 攻略テキスト」がこの *Seize the Core of the TOEIC Test* というわけです。以下にその特徴と使い方をまとめていますので、うまく使いこなし、ぜひともスコアアップに役立ててください。

## 1．「内容に関するテーマ」と Key Vocabulary

　各ユニットに、TOEIC 頻出の場面を想定した「内容に関するテーマ」を設定しています。また、巻末には、そのテーマ特有の頻出語句を集めた Key Vocabulary が収録されています。本テキストの問題は、この Key Vocabulary の語句を繰り返し用いながら「内容に関するテーマ」に沿って作成されていますので、問題を解き進めるうちに、頻出の場面設定と頻出語句を自然に学ぶことができます。Key Vocabulary はとにかく実践を意識して作成していますので、しっかり覚えて身に付ければ教科書や授業内容の理解に大いに役立つだけでなく、実際のスコアアップにかなりの効果が期待できます。

## 2．習得すべき頻出「文法テーマ」

　各ユニットには「内容に関するテーマ」と並行して、習得すべき頻出「文法テーマ」を設定しています。文法は、ただ問題をやみくもに解くよりも、テーマごとに知識を整理しながら出題傾向に合わせた練習をするのが最も効果的です。リーディングのみならず、リスニング問題もこの「文法テーマ」に沿って作成されていますので、中高で学んだ文法事項を復習しながら、TOEIC 頻出の文法ポイントを効率よく押さえていきましょう。

## 3．「ターゲット」と「解法のポイント」

　すべてのパートに、TOEIC の問題パターンを意識した「ターゲット」と「解法のポイント」を設定し、「TOEIC に慣れるためのカギ」を分かりやすく解説していま

す。「ターゲット」ではTOEIC独特の出題パターンについて紹介し、「解法のポイント」では具体的なアドバイスが提示されています。それぞれのパートの頻出パターン、解答者が陥りやすい間違いなど、スコアアップに役立つヒントがぎっしり詰まっています。同じ間違いを繰り返しながら、やみくもに問題を解き進めていくのではなく、それらのヒントしっかり活かして、効率的に勉強していきましょう。

### 4．音声データのダウンロード

　本テキストの音声データはダウンロードして入手することができます（IntroductionとReview Testを除く）。それらを最大限に活用すれば、リスニング用の問題集を買う必要はありません。音声を音楽デバイスなどにダウンロードして、毎日1ユニットずつ聞きましょう。音声のスピードは実際のTOEICよりも若干遅めに設定されていますので、耳を慣らす練習にはうってつけです。授業の予習・復習に役立つのはもちろんのこと、頻出語句の正しい発音や英語独特のイントネーションを浴びて耳を鍛えることで、本番での確実なスコアアップが期待できます。

　また、ダウンロード音声を繰り返し聞いて耳が慣れてきたところで、本当に聞き取れているか確認するために、ディクテーション（音声を聞いて英語を書き取る）の練習をお勧めします。何となく正解できているけれども、正確な聞き取りに自信がないという場合は、ディクテーションで再確認して、リスニング力の精度を上げましょう。

### 5．Review Test［復習テスト］

　本テキストには、前半ユニット（Unit 1～6）の復習用としてReview Test 1を、また後半ユニット（Unit 7～12）の復習用としてReview Test 2を用意しています。これらのReview Testは、対象範囲の学習内容が着実に身に付いているかを確認するための復習応用問題です。このテストで好成績を上げるためには、各ユニットを学習する際にただ答えを暗記するのではなく、その答えに至る過程と理由をきちんと理解することが大切です。前半・後半それぞれの復習を行って、本物の実力を付けましょう。巻末にはReview Test用の切り取り式解答用マークシートも用意しています。

### 6．全体の構成

　1回（90分）の授業で取り組めるよう、各ユニットにつき4つのパートを取りあげ、バランス良くコンパクトに構成されています。Part 1, 7は全ユニットで、Part 2, 3, 4はそれぞれ3ユニットに一度、Part 5はUnit 4, 8, 12を除くすべてのユニットで、Part 6はUnit 4, 8, 12でそれぞれ扱っています。詳しくは、Contentsを参照してください。

　最後に、本テキストの刊行にあたり、前作に引き続き金星堂の皆様には大変お世話になりました。この場を借りてお礼申し上げます。

著者一同

# 本書は CheckLink（チェックリンク）対応テキストです。

CheckLinkのアイコンが表示されている設問は、CheckLinkに対応しています。
CheckLinkを使用しなくても従来通りの授業ができますが、特色をご理解いただき、授業活性化のためにぜひご活用ください。

## CheckLinkの特色について

　大掛かりで複雑な従来のe-learningシステムとは異なり、CheckLinkのシステムは大きな特色として次の3点が挙げられます。
1. これまで行われてきた教科書を使った授業展開に大幅な変化を加えることなく、専門的な知識なしにデジタル学習環境を導入することができる。
2. PC教室やCALL教室といった最新の機器が導入された教室に限定されることなく、普通教室を使用した授業でもデジタル学習環境を導入することができる。
3. 授業中での使用に特化し、教師・学習者双方のモチベーション・集中力をアップさせ、授業自体を活性化することができる。

### ▶教科書を使用した授業に「デジタル学習環境」を導入できる

　本システムでは、学習者は教科書のCheckLinkのアイコンが表示されている設問にPCやスマートフォン、携帯電話端末からインターネットを通して解答します。そして教師は、授業中にリアルタイムで解答結果を把握し、正解率などに応じて有効な解説を行うことができるようになっています。教科書自体は従来と何ら変わりはありません。解答の手段としてCheckLinkを使用しない場合でも、従来通りの教科書として使用して授業を行うことも、もちろん可能です。

### ▶教室環境を選ばない

　従来の多機能なe-learning教材のように学習者側の画面に多くの機能を持たせることはせず、「解答する」ことに機能を特化しました。PCだけでなく、一部タブレット端末やスマートフォン、携帯電話端末からの解答も可能です。したがって、PC教室やCALL教室といった大掛かりな教室は必要としません。普通教室でもCheckLinkを用いた授業が可能です。教師はPCだけでなく、一部タブレット端末やスマートフォンからも解答結果の確認をすることができます。

### ▶授業を活性化するための支援システム

　本システムは予習や復習のツールとしてではなく、授業中に活用されることで真価を発揮する仕組みになっています。CheckLinkというデジタル学習環境を通じ、教師と学習者双方が授業中に解答状況などの様々な情報を共有することで、学習者はやる気を持って解答し、教師は解答状況に応じて効果的な解説を行う、という好循環を生み出します。CheckLinkは、普段の授業をより活力のあるものへと変えていきます。

　上記3つの大きな特色以外にも、掲示板などの授業中に活用できる機能を用意しています。従来通りの教科書としても使用はできますが、ぜひCheckLinkの機能をご理解いただき、普段の授業をより活性化されたものにしていくためにご活用ください。

# CheckLink の使い方

CheckLinkは、PCや一部タブレット端末、スマートフォン、携帯電話端末を用いて、この教科書の ↻CheckLink のアイコン表示のある設問に解答するシステムです。
・初めてCheckLinkを使う場合、以下の要領で**「学習者登録」**と**「教科書登録」**を行います。
・一度登録を済ませれば、あとは毎回**「ログイン画面」**から入るだけです。CheckLinkを使う教科書が増えたときだけ、改めて**「教科書登録」**を行ってください。

**CheckLink URL**

https://checklink.kinsei-do.co.jp/student/

QRコードの読み取りができる端末の場合はこちらから ▶▶▶

ご注意ください！ 上記URLは**「検索ボックス」**でなく**「アドレスバー(URL表示欄)」**に入力してください。

## ▶学習者登録

①上記URLにアクセスすると、右のページが表示されます。学校名を入力し「ログイン画面へ」をクリックしてください。
**PCの場合は「PC用はこちら」をクリックして**PC用ページを表示します。同様に学校名を入力し「ログイン画面へ」をクリックしてください。

②ログイン画面が表示されたら**「初めての方はこちら」**をクリックし「学習者登録画面」に入ります。

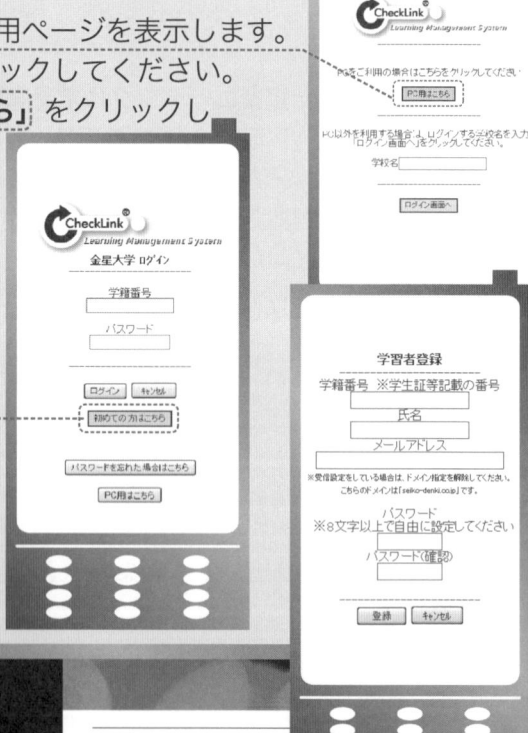

③自分の学籍番号、氏名、メールアドレス（学校のメールなど**PCメールを推奨**）を入力し、次に**任意のパスワード**を8桁以上20桁未満（半角英数字）で入力します。なお、学籍番号はパスワードとして使用することはできません。

④「パスワード確認」は、❸で入力したパスワードと同じものを入力します。

⑤最後に「登録」ボタンをクリックして登録は完了です。次回からは、「ログイン画面」から学籍番号とパスワードを入力してログインしてください。

## ▶教科書登録

①ログイン後、メニュー画面から「教科書登録」を選び（PCの場合はその後「新規登録」ボタンをクリック）、「教科書登録」画面を開きます。

②教科書と受講する授業を登録します。
教科書の最終ページにある、**教科書固有番号**のシールをはがし、印字された**16桁の数字とアルファベット**を入力します。

③授業を担当される先生から連絡された**11桁の授業ID**を入力します。

④最後に「登録」ボタンをクリックして登録は完了です。

⑤実際に使用する際は「教科書一覧」（PCの場合は「教科書選択画面」）の該当する教科書名をクリックすると、「問題解答」の画面が表示されます。

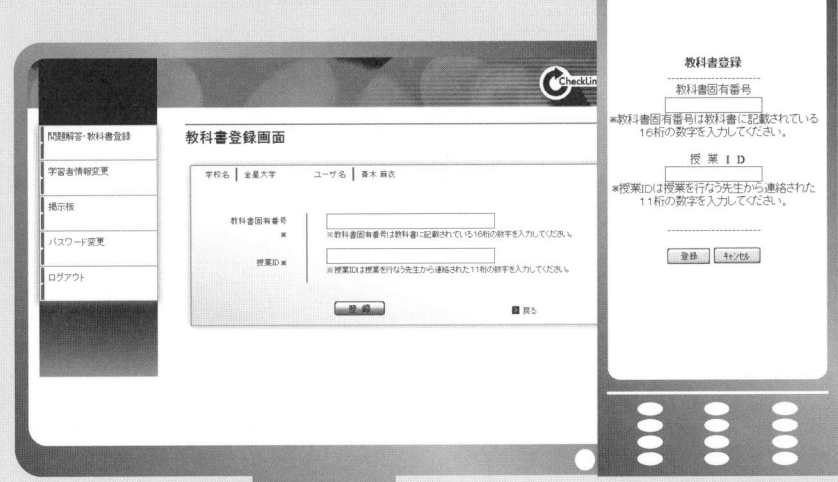

## ▶問題解答

①問題は教科書を見ながら解答します。この教科書の CheckLink のアイコン表示のある設問に解答できます。

②問題が表示されたら選択肢を選びます。

③表示されている問題に解答した後、「解答」ボタンをクリックすると解答が登録されます。

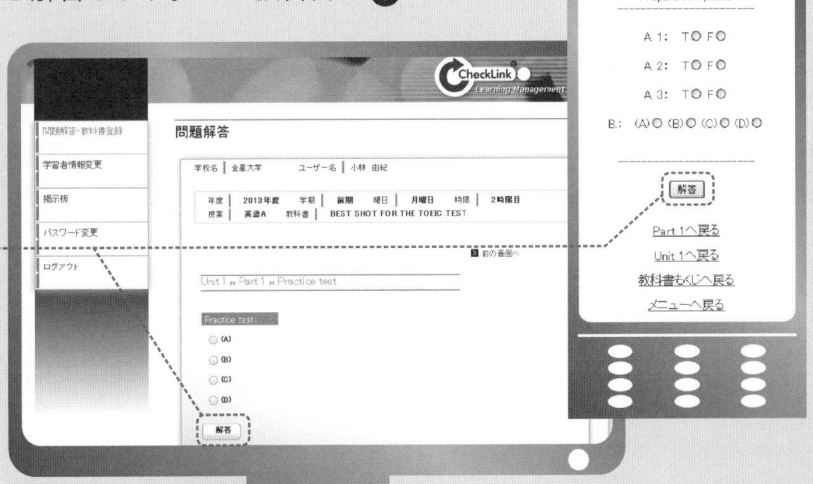

▶**CheckLink 推奨環境**

**PC**

推奨 OS
  Windows XP, Vista 以降
  Macintosh OS X 以降
  Linux

推奨ブラウザ
  Internet Explorer 6.0 以上
  Firefox 3.0 以上
  Safari
  Opera
  Google Chrome

**携帯電話・スマートフォン**

3G 以降の携帯電話（docomo, au, softbank）
iPhone, iPad
Android OS スマートフォン、タブレット

▶**CheckLink 開発**

CheckLink は奥田裕司 福岡大学教授、正興 IT ソリューション株式会社、株式会社金星堂によって共同開発されました。

CheckLink は株式会社金星堂の登録商標です。

---

**CheckLink の使い方に関するお問い合わせは…**

正興ITソリューション株式会社　CheckLink 係

**e-mail**　checklink@seiko-denki.co.jp

# Contents

**SEIZE THE CORE OF THE TOEIC® TEST**

本テキストの特徴とその使い方
CheckLink について
TOEIC テストについて

**Introduction** ─────────────────── 14

## Unit 1  Daily Life ［基本 5 文型］ ─────────── 20
- Part 1　写真に何が写っているかをよく見よう
- Part 2　似た音や連想される語に飛びつかない
- Part 5　基本 5 文型をマスターしよう
- Part 7　取扱説明書に慣れよう

## Unit 2  Eating Out & Leisure Activities ［品詞］ ─── 26
- Part 1　すべての選択肢を最後まで聞こう
- Part 3　会話の全体的な流れを把握しよう
- Part 5　品詞の見分け方をマスターしよう
- Part 7　スキャニングをマスターしよう

## Unit 3  Cooking & Purchasing ［名詞・主語と動詞の一致］ ─── 32
- Part 1　人物の「動作」に注目しよう
- Part 4　客に向けたアナウンスに慣れよう
- Part 5　名詞と、主語と動詞の呼応関係をマスターしよう
- Part 7　広告・宣伝の形式に慣れよう

## Unit 4  Traffic & Travel ［形容詞・副詞］ ───── 38
- Part 1　人物が写っていない写真問題に慣れよう
- Part 2　WH 疑問文に慣れよう
- Part 6　形容詞と副詞の働きをマスターしよう
- Part 7　告知文書に慣れよう

## Unit 5  Advertising & ICT ［時制］ ──────── 44
- Part 1　動詞の時制を聞き取ろう
- Part 3　質問と選択肢を先に読もう
- Part 5　時制をマスターしよう
- Part 7　スキミングをマスターしよう

## Unit 6  Production & Logistics ［接続詞・前置詞］ ─── 50
- Part 1　類義語や言い換えに注意しよう
- Part 4　「誰に向かって話しているのか」をつかもう
- Part 5　接続詞と前置詞をマスターしよう
- Part 7　記事に慣れよう

**Review Test 1** ───────────────── 56

## Unit 7    Business & Economics ［助動詞］ ———————— 64

Part 1　人や物の位置関係を正確にとらえよう
Part 2　質問ではない疑問文に慣れよう
Part 5　助動詞をマスターしよう
Part 7　手紙やメールに慣れよう

## Unit 8    Employment & Personnel ［受動態］ ———————— 70

Part 1　受動態の表現に慣れよう
Part 3　日常生活やビジネスの現場で使用される単語・表現を覚えておこう
Part 6　受動態をマスターしよう
Part 7　ビジネス文書に慣れよう①

## Unit 9    Office Work & Correspondence ［分詞・分詞構文］ ———————— 76

Part 1　発音が同じ単語や表現に注意しよう
Part 4　留守番電話に慣れよう
Part 5　分詞と分詞構文をマスターしよう
Part 7　ビジネス文書に慣れよう②

## Unit 10    Health & the Environment ［不定詞・動名詞］ ———————— 82

Part 1　発音が似ている単語に注意しよう
Part 2　変則的な応答問題に注意しよう
Part 5　不定詞と動名詞をマスターしよう
Part 7　速読力をつけよう

## Unit 11    Finance & Banking ［代名詞・関係詞］ ———————— 88

Part 1　多義語に注意しよう
Part 3　長文のリスニングに慣れよう
Part 5　代名詞の用法を確認して、関係代名詞と関係副詞をマスターしよう
Part 7　通知文書に慣れよう

## Unit 12    Law & Administration ［比較構文］ ———————— 94

Part 1　専門用語に慣れよう
Part 4　報道・ニュースに慣れよう
Part 6　比較構文をマスターしよう
Part 7　色々な種類の英文を読もう

**Review Test 2** ———————— 100

Key Vocabulary (Unit 1-12)
Review Test マークシート

# TOEIC テストについて

TOEIC テストはリスニングとリーディングの2つのセクションで構成されていて、全部で200問あります。Introduction を始める前に、7つのパートの問題形式について確認しましょう。

## リスニングセクション　45分

### Part 1　Photographs　写真描写問題　10問

1枚の写真について、4つの説明文（A）〜（D）が放送されます。4つの説明文のうち、写真を最も適切に描写しているものを選択します。説明文は問題用紙に印刷されていません。また、音声は一度しか放送されません。

―― サンプル問題 ――――――――――――――――――――――――――

1. (A) A woman is walking a dog.
　 (B) A woman is riding a bicycle.
　 (C) A woman is entering a house.
　 (D) A woman is looking out of the window.

　　　　　　　　　　―― 音声のみ・印刷なし

### Part 2　Question - Response　応答問題　30問

1つの問いかけが放送された後、問いかけに対する3つの応答（A）〜（C）が放送され、応答として最も適切なものを選択します。問いかけも応答も問題用紙に印刷されていません。また、音声は一度しか放送されません。

―― サンプル問題 ――――――――――――――――――――――――――

11. How often do you exercise?　　　　―― 音声のみ・印刷なし
　 (A) Yes, I like exercising so much.
　 (B) Once or twice a week.
　 (C) My brother teaches me how to exercise.

# Part 3 Conversations　会話問題　30問（1つの会話＋3つの設問が10セット）

2人の人物の会話を聞き、問題用紙に印刷されている3つの設問と4つの選択肢（A）〜（D）を読んで、解答として最も適切なものを選択します。会話は放送のみで、印刷されていません。3つの設問は放送されますが、4つの選択肢（A）〜（D）は放送されません。また、音声は一度しか放送されません。

――― サンプル問題 ―――

M: Excuse me, could you tell me the way to the nearest train station from this hotel?

W: Certainly. Here is a free map for our guests. Where are you going? There are several stations around this hotel.

M: I see. I have a conference to attend at Park Hall. I was told to get off the train at Green Park Station.

W: In that case, Albert Station will give you good access to Green Park Station. Its entrance is on the opposite side of this hotel.

41. Where most likely are the speakers?　　　　　　　── 音声のみ・印刷なし
　　(A) At a station　　　　　── 音声も印刷もあり
　　(B) At a hotel
　　(C) At a conference
　　(D) At Park Hall　　　　　　　　　　　　　　　　　1セット全3問

# Part 4 Talks　説明文問題　30問（1つの説明文＋3つの設問が10セット）

やや長めの説明文を聞き、問題用紙に印刷されている3つの設問と4つの選択肢（A）〜（D）を読んで、解答として最も適切なものを選択します。説明文は放送のみで、印刷されていません。3つの設問は放送されますが、4つの選択肢（A）〜（D）は放送されません。また、音声は一度しか放送されません。

――― サンプル問題 ―――

Sydney Marine Zoo is pleased to announce its first ever Sea Animal Photo Contest. The contest is open to all ages, and cash prizes will be awarded in three categories. Photographers are invited to submit online their photographs of tropical fish at home, sea animals in the wild and friends at Sydney Marine Zoo. The deadline for the contest is 11:59 PM, just before midnight, on March 15th. Enter today!

71. What is the main purpose of this announcement?　── 音声のみ・印刷なし
　　(A) To welcome new animals　　── 音声も印刷もあり
　　(B) To post a job vacancy
　　(C) To request donations online
　　(D) To release information about a contest　　　　1セット全3問

# リーディングセクション　75分

## Part 5　Incomplete Sentences　短文穴埋め問題　40問

空所が1つある不完全な英文を完成させるために、4つの選択肢（A）〜（D）の中から最も適切なものを選択します。

---
**サンプル問題**

**101.** Basic ------- for the job include a college degree, good work experience and an energetic personality.
(A) qualifications
(B) qualifying
(C) qualify
(D) qualified

---

## Part 6　Text Completion　長文穴埋め問題　12問
（1つの文章＋3つの設問が4セット）

空所が3つある不完全な文書を完成させるために、それぞれ4つの選択肢（A）〜（D）の中から最も適切なものを選択します。

---
**サンプル問題**

**FIRE SAFETY EVACUATION PLAN**

We have developed an evacuation plan for employees to use during emergency situations. Each employee is ------- to maintain an updated copy of the plan and be

**141.** (A) replayed
(B) reached
(C) remoted
(D) requested

prepared to properly respond in the event of an emergency situation.

An alert and educated staff is our company's most valuable resource for fire protection. Fire hazards arise from unsafe conditions and practices. Every employee has a responsibility and vested interest in making a concerted…

1セット全3問

# Part 7 Reading Comprehension  読解問題  48問
（9個の Single Passage で28問＋4セットの Double Passage で20問）

さまざまな内容の文書を読み、その内容に関する設問に対してそれぞれ4つの選択肢（A）〜（D）の中から最も適切なものを選択します。広告やオフィスメモなどの<u>1つの文書</u>（Single Passage）を読んで解答する設問が28問、メールのやり取りなど<u>2つで1セットの文書</u>（Double Passage）を読んで解答する設問が20問あります。

---
**サンプル問題**

## Kevin's Burgers

45 Rockland Way, Seattle, Washington 98133   (206) 359-5814

We're celebrating our 30th anniversary this spring!
Present this coupon and receive…
## ONE FREE Kevin's Special Burger
with the purchase of a regular burger

Valid until May 31. One coupon per customer visit. Not valid with any other discounts or offers.

---

**153.** What is NOT mentioned in this advertisement?
  (A) Kevin's birthday
  (B) Special offer
  (C) Expiration date
  (D) Location of the shop

**154.** How can the coupon be used?
  (A) By presenting more than two coupons
  (B) By visiting Kevin's house
  (C) By receiving a special gift
  (D) By buying a regular burger

1セット全2〜5問

# Introduction

## Part 1

 CheckLink  CD1-02

Look at the picture and choose the statement that best describes what you see in the picture.

**1.**

(A)　(B)　(C)　(D)

**2.**

(A)　(B)　(C)　(D)

# Part 2

Listen to the question or statement and the three responses. Then choose the best response to each question or statement.

3. (A)   (B)   (C)
4. (A)   (B)   (C)
5. (A)   (B)   (C)

# Part 3

Listen to the conversation and choose the best answer to each question.

6. Who is the woman?
   (A) The man's colleague
   (B) The man's wife
   (C) A waitress
   (D) A cook

7. What would the man like to order?
   (A) Chicken
   (B) French dressing
   (C) Dessert
   (D) Steak

8. What will the woman probably do next?
   (A) Show the menu
   (B) Bring beer
   (C) Take the man's order
   (D) Clean up the table

## Part 4

Listen to the short talk and choose the best answer to each question.

9. Who most likely are the listeners?
   (A) Customers
   (B) Passengers
   (C) Tour guides
   (D) Factory workers

10. When can listeners ask a question by phone?
    (A) At 9 a.m. on Monday
    (B) At 4 p.m. on Tuesday
    (C) At 10 a.m. on Saturday
    (D) At 6 p.m. on Sunday

11. Why would listeners press "0"?
    (A) To leave a message in voice mail
    (B) To make a reservation for a tour
    (C) To repeat the recording
    (D) To end the call

## Part 5

Choose the best answer to complete the sentence.

12. Because I exceeded the speed limit by thirty kilometers, I had to pay a $100 ------- for speeding.
    (A) fare     (B) cost     (C) fine     (D) price

13. The pharmaceutical representative told us that their new medication would be quite ------- in the treatment of cancer.
    (A) affect     (B) effective     (C) affection     (D) effectively

14. A monthly sales report needs to be submitted ------- the end of the month.
    (A) by     (B) to     (C) by the time     (D) until

# Part 6

**Questions 15-17** refer to the following e-mail.

From: ZEUS Customer Service
To: Jason Berners
Subject: RE: the SuperPrint 4000

Mr. Berners:

Thank you very much for your inquiry about our new product, the SuperPrint 4000, the all-in-one printer. The SuperPrint 4000 newly features wireless connectivity. Connecting through Wi-Fi allows you to print directly from mobile devices. -------, this model saves you time, space and money. It takes

    **15.** (A) However
        (B) Moreover
        (C) Nevertheless
        (D) Otherwise

only 50 seconds to print 40 pages, is the same size as an average Blu-ray player and offers cost-effective printing ------- individual inks.

    **16.** (A) according to
        (B) but for
        (C) instead of
        (D) thanks to

It also has an auto-document feeder and functions as a copier and high resolution scanner. This new model would definitely ------- your needs.

    **17.** (A) satisfaction
        (B) satisfy
        (C) satisfied
        (D) to satisfy

Please find attached the file with the specifications and the price list. If you have any questions, please do not hesitate to contact us. Thank you for your interest in our product.

Sincerely yours,

Janie Smith
ZEUS Customer Service

# Part 7

**Questions 18-20** refer to the following advertisement.

# New Store Opening

## Frankie's Five Fabulicious Fruity Flavors
Gardenside Plaza
4528 Willing Drive
www.Frankies5.com

*Frankie* - the handsome owner serving you
*Five* - the number of flavors to sample in the sampler pack
*Fabulicious* - how you will describe the taste of our ice cream
*Fruity* - the overall sensation you'll get in your mouth
*Flavors* - Apple Candy, Citrus Delight, Melon Magic, Swinging Banana, Zany Berries

Looking for some excitement in your ice cream? Come taste our five fruity flavors. Nothing cooler, nothing tastier. Guaranteed to get your taste buds tingling.

**Opening on Friday, June 1, just in time for the heat of summer.**

**Open Wednesday through Monday from 9 a.m. to 10 p.m.**
Be one of the first 30 customers to enter the store on June 1
and get a free small cone with any order.

----------------------------- *coupon* -----------------------------

Present this coupon at the time of your order and receive a complimentary sampler pack. Valid with any order over $10. Limited to one coupon per order.
(Offer valid for the whole month of June.)

**18.** How many samples are in the sampler pack?
   (A) One     (B) Two     (C) Four     (D) Five

**19.** Which day is the store closed?
   (A) Monday     (B) Tuesday     (C) Thursday     (D) Sunday

**20.** When do you receive a sampler pack?
   (A) When you buy more than $10 worth of product and present the coupon
   (B) At the time of order
   (C) When you come to the store in June
   (D) When you are one of the first 30 customers to enter the store

# 今の大学生にとって必要なTOEICテスト
## その勉強をすることの意味とは

　TOEICテストのスコアは、採用試験では応募者の英語能力を測るものとして、また企業では社員の昇進・昇格や海外出張・駐在の要件として広く採用されています。その理由として、①他の英語の資格試験と比べて安価である、②試験回数が多く受験しやすい、③幅のある級ではなくスコアで英語力を測ることができる、などが挙げられ、就職活動を控えた学生だけでなく、多くの社会人もTOEICのスコアアップを目指して日々勉強をしています。

### 中高で学んだ内容＋αが求められるテスト

　TOEICテストはリスニングとリーディングの2つのセクションで構成され、扱われている内容は日常の場面からビジネスまで多岐にわたります。リスニングでは職場での会話や飛行機などの交通機関の案内、リーディングではレストランのメニューやさまざまな広告、時刻表や社内文書などがあり、中高での授業では接する機会が少なかった分野に関する内容が多くなります。スコアアップを目指すには、まず、これまでに学んだ英単語に加えて、そういった分野の語彙を増やさなければなりません。

　また、特にリーディングセクションでは、正確な英文法の知識も求められます。TOEICテストにおける文法の知識を問う問題は、高校や大学の入学試験のものとは異なります。それらに対応できる力を身につけるためにも、大学生としてのより一歩進んだ幅広い文法の勉強が必要になってきます。

### TOEICのための勉強を総合的な英語力につなげる

　TOEICテストは2時間で200問の問題に挑む、集中力を要するテストです。最初のうちは、問題の音声を十分に聞きとることができずに次の問題が始まってしまったり、読解問題の時間が足りずに終了時間が来てしまったりする受験生もいることでしょう。日常的な場面や不慣れなビジネスに関するかなりの量の英語を聞いて読んで、瞬間的に理解するのは容易なことではありません。そのためには、とにかく英語をたくさん聞いて読んで、地道に練習することが欠かせません。

　こうしたTOEICテストのための勉強を続ければ、リスニング・リーディング・語彙・文法のスキルが確実に伸びてきます。TOEICのスコアは総合的な英語力を証明するものではありませんので、必ずしも「スコアが高いから英語が堪能」ということにはなりません。しかし、総合的な力の向上には、リスニング・リーディング力や文法の知識、さらに語彙力も絶対に必要で、それらが十分にあるか無いかで、成果の出るスピードに大きな差が出てくるのも事実です。つまり、TOEICへの取り組みは、単なる資格や評価の取得にとどまらない、総合的な英語力の土台を育てることにつながるのです。そして、勉強法を工夫して計画を立てたり、それを実施するために努力を続けたりすることを通して、広い意味で問題解決能力や自己管理能力も育むことができるでしょう。

　就職のために勉強をする、というのが最も分かりやすくてシンプルな理由かもしれません。しかし、せっかく今回TOEICの勉強をするのですから、その過程で培われたリスニングやリーディングの力をベースに、会話力や表現力もアップさせて、ぜひ海外旅行や語学研修、留学などに積極的に挑戦してみてください。

# Unit 1 Daily Life

## Part 1 ターゲット 写真に何が写っているかをよく見よう

Part 1 の問題では写真に何が描写されているかが問われるので、写真に写っているものだけが正解になる。写真に写っていないものはもちろん、想像力を働かせた描写や推測しなければならない選択肢は迷わず排除してよい。とにかく写真をしっかり見て解答することを心がけよう。

Listen and fill in the blanks for each sentence. Then choose the statement that best describes what you see in the picture.

1.   CheckLink  DL 02  CD1-06 ~ CD1-10

(A) A woman is (　　　　　) a ceiling
　　(　　　) (　　　　　) in the kitchen.
(B) A woman is (　　　　) a
　　(　　　　) (　　　).
(C) A woman is (　　　　　) a
　　(　　　　　　　) shirt.
(D) A woman is (　　　　　) a
　　(　　　　　) (　　　).

Choose the statement that best describes what you see in the picture.

2.   CheckLink  DL 03  CD1-11

(A)　(B)　(C)　(D)

## 解法のポイント　語彙を増やして、英語表現に慣れる

せっかく写真に写っている対象を正確にとらえても、英語ではどのように表現するのかを知らなければ、正答にはたどり着けない。例えば「オーブンレンジ」が見えたとしても、それが英語では microwave oven となることを知らなければ、正しい選択肢を選べなくなってしまう。語彙を増やす努力をし、普段から身の回りのものを英語ではどう表現するのかを意識して欲しい。

# Part 2  似た音や連想される語に飛びつかない

質問中に使われている単語、音が似ている単語、テーマと関連のありそうな単語が流れてきても、すぐには飛びつかないで、すべての選択肢を最後まで聞いてから、落ち着いて答えを選ぶようにしよう。

Listen and fill in the blanks for each sentence. Then choose the best response to each question or statement.  CheckLink  DL 04 ~ 06  CD1-12
CD1-13 ~ CD1-16

1. Will you (     ) these (        ) on that table?
    (A) I'm (        ) (      ) the tables (       ) (         ).
    (B) Sure, (        ) (       ).
    (C) The books you (         ) (        ) in the top (         ).

CD1-17 ~ CD1-20

2. Where should we (      ) (      ) (        ) honeymoon?
    (A) We (        ) (        ) (            ) for five years.
    (B) We stayed (        ) a (        ) (         ) room with a big balcony.
    (C) I'd (        ) (       ) (         ) to Australia.

CD1-21 ~ CD1-24

3. Do you have _____?
    (A) I'm sorry. _____.
    (B) _____.
    (C) The store is _____.

Listen to the question or statement and the three responses. Then choose the best response.

4. (A)    (B)    (C)       CheckLink   DL 07   CD1-25

### 解法のポイント　　「いかにも」な選択肢は危険

質問中に使われている単語、音が似ている単語、テーマと関連のありそうな単語が露骨に使われている、そういった「いかにも」な選択肢こそ、実は「引っかけ」である確率が高いので、むしろ警戒した方が良い。

Unit 1 Daily Life ○ 21

# Part 5  基本５文型をマスターしよう

**Choose the best answer to complete the sentence.**

**1.** 第１文型：Every morning Ms. Henderson ------- by train all the way to her office in Yokohama.
   (A) visits
   (B) leaves
   (C) commutes
   (D) works

**2.** 第１文型：She went ------- to take the clothes out of the washer and put them into the drier.
   (A) stairs
   (B) downstairs
   (C) the first floor
   (D) steps

**3.** 第２文型：The rainy season in Japan is so ------- that the laundry won't dry.
   (A) humidify
   (B) humidity
   (C) humiliate
   (D) humid

**4.** 第２文型：I found a condo that looked really ------- and seemed affordable, so I signed a contract to buy it.
   (A) comfortable
   (B) comfortably
   (C) comfort
   (D) comforter

**5.** 第３文型：This newly released detergent is so strong that it can ------- delicate fabrics.
   (A) damage
   (B) damageable
   (C) damagingly
   (D) damaged

**6.** 第３文型：A blackout, caused by an accident at the power plant which supplies electricity to the suburb, ------- about six hundred thousand households.
   (A) effectively
   (B) affected
   (C) fluency
   (D) influential

**7.** 第 4 文型：My master plumber identified the leak, told me to pass him his tools and showed ------- to fix it.
　(A) mine the way　　　(C) my to the way
　(B) the way of me　　　(D) me the way

**8.** 第 4 文型：The landlord ------- the tenant that his monthly rent includes the utilities.
　(A) said　　　(C) told
　(B) mentioned　　　(D) remarked

**9.** 第 5 文型：They ------- the skyscraper the Empire State Building after the state of New York's nickname.
　(A) created　　　(C) kept
　(B) named　　　(D) built

**10.** 第 5 文型：The police made all the residents ------- the region because of the possibility of a gas explosion.
　(A) to evacuate　　　(C) evacuate
　(B) evacuating　　　(D) onto being evacuated

 解法のポイント　　構造に注意する習慣を身に付ける　

文法問題では、和訳につられてしまう恐れがあるため、訳してから解答を探す方法はおススメしない。まず文型や文構造に注意して、空所に入る語がどのような文法的役割を担っているのかを考えて、選択肢を絞ってから答えを出す、というのが基本の解き方だ。

Unit 1　Daily Life　23

# Part 7  取扱説明書に慣れよう

取扱説明書には、商品の特性、使用方法、注意事項などが書いてある。TOEIC の取扱説明書は常識的な内容のものがほとんどなので、パターンに慣れて、短時間で解けるようにしよう。

**Questions 1-4** refer to the following instructions.

**Our new and improved detergent pacs will make your laundry cleaner than new.**
**Read and follow these instructions for best results.**

1. Sort your washable clothing. Separate the dark colors from the light colors and whites.
2. Adjust the color settings on your washing machine for the appropriate color type.
3. For best results, check that the temperature setting is on cool or cold water for dark colors, and cool or warm water for light colors and whites. When in doubt, refer to the care label on your clothing for specific instructions.
4. Put the clothing into the machine.
5. Add detergent pacs directly into the machine with your laundry. Do not put the pacs in the detergent drawer.
6. Use the following guide for the correct amount of detergent.
   small load: 2 pacs
   regular load: 3 pacs
   large load: 4 pacs
7. Start your washing machine.

**Warning:**
 - **Only use with laundry appliances.**
 - **Avoid overloading the machine.**
 - **Do not use more than 4 pacs at once.** For extra dirty laundry, it is suggested to pre-soak clothes before washing.

1. What is the purpose of the information?
   (A) To explain how to choose the best washing machine
   (B) To explain how to clean the washing machine
   (C) To explain how to use the detergent
   (D) To explain how to do the laundry

2. What should we NOT do?
   (A) Set the temperature to warm for whites
   (B) Mix dark colors and light colors
   (C) Add the detergent pacs with the laundry
   (D) Avoid putting too many clothes in the machine

3. How many detergent pacs should we use if we have a lot of laundry?
   (A) Three
   (B) Four
   (C) Five
   (D) Six

4. Which type of clothes should be washed using cool water?
   (A) Dark colors
   (B) Light colors
   (C) Whites
   (D) All of the above

  導入文を必ず読むこと

Part 7 では本文の上（枠外）にある導入文に注目。そこには、letter, notice, advertisement, chart, memorandum など、これから読む文章がどのような形式なのかが一言で要約されている。ここに必ず目を通し、文章の種類に合わせて心の準備をしておくと、必要な情報を見つけやすくなる。

# Unit 2 Eating Out & Leisure Activities

## Part 1 ターゲット　すべての選択肢を最後まで聞こう

Part 1では写真に写っている人・物・状況について尋ねられるが、写っていない人や物について述べている文は、もちろん正解にはならない。ただし、写真に写っている人物や物などを主語にした文が聞こえたからといって、必ずしもそれが正解というわけではないので注意が必要だ。

Listen and fill in the blanks for each sentence. Then choose the statement that best describes what you see in the picture.

1.

   DL 08　CD1-26 ~ CD1-30

   (A) A customer is (　　　　)
   　　(　　) the counter.
   (B) The diner is (　　　　)
   　　Mexican (　　).
   (C) Employees are (　　　　)
   　　(　　　　　) the customers.
   (D) The counter has (　　　)
   　　(　　　　　) with stools.

Choose the statement that best describes what you see in the picture.

2. CheckLink　DL 09　CD1-31

   (A)　(B)　(C)　(D)

### 解法のポイント　写真に写っている語が聞こえても飛びつかない

写真に写っている人や物を主語とする文が読み上げられても、最後まで聞かなければ正解かどうか判断できない。例えば、座っている男性が写真に写っていて、The man ~ で始まる文が聞こえたとしても、The man is sleeping ~ と続けば当然不正解である。それらしい単語に安易に飛びつかないで、落ち着いて最後まで聞くこと。

# Part 3  会話の全体的な流れを把握しよう

受験者が会話を全体的に把握できているかどうかを試すために、「2人が話している話題は何か」という質問は頻繁に出題される。まず、「何が話されているのか」を理解し、全体の流れを把握しよう。

Listen to the conversation and fill in the blanks. Then choose the best answer to each question.  CheckLink  DL 10  CD1-32 ~ CD1-36

M: I want to (1.        ) (2.        ) for the (3.        ) next month. (4.        ) can I get them?

W: You can (5.        ) tickets (6.        ) (7.        ) at our box office. You can also (8.        ) tickets by phone.

M: Can I book by phone and (9.        ) (10.        ) the tickets on the day of the (11.        )?

W: Yes. You must (12.        ) the credit card you used for your order, a (13.        ) (14.        ) ID card, and the (15.        ) (16.        ) at the box office.

1. What are the speakers talking about?  DL 11  CD1-37
   (A) Buying books online
   (B) Teleshopping
   (C) Booking tickets
   (D) Box office performances

2. How will the man probably purchase the tickets?
   (A) By telephone
   (B) Online
   (C) By mail order
   (D) At the ticket office

3. What does the woman tell the man to do at the box office?
   (A) Take a photo of himself
   (B) Show the credit card he used to purchase the tickets
   (C) Confirm his seat reservation
   (D) Pay for the tickets in cash

Listen to the conversation and choose the best answer to each question.

4. What are the speakers discussing?
   (A) Where to hold a party
   (B) How to find party-goers
   (C) When to start a party
   (D) Why Nancy didn't like the dessert

5. How many people will the man ask to attend the party?
   (A) More than 15 people
   (B) About a dozen people
   (C) More than 50 people
   (D) He hasn't decided.

6. What does the woman recommend?
   (A) Holding a wedding banquet for Nancy
   (B) Using dessert coupons
   (C) Wearing casual clothes at the party
   (D) Using the restaurant the speakers used before

---

解法のポイント　　　２人の関係に注意　　　

Part 3は、男性と女性が交互に話すパターンである。会話の内容だけでなく、口調や抑揚にも注意して２人の関係を推測し、どのような会話が展開されているか把握したい。

　　品詞の見分け方をマスターしよう　　

Choose the best answer to complete the sentence.

1. 名詞：Her ------- was so convincing and impressive that the audience showered her with applause.
   (A) perform  (B) performable  (C) performers  (D) performance

2. 名詞：You should make a ------- beforehand if you don't want to wait for hours because that restaurant is extremely popular now.
   (A) preserve  (B) preservative  (C) reservation  (D) reservoir

3. 名詞：Some modern people regard playing golf as a leisure ------- or an opportunity to develop a network of business contacts, not just as a sport.
   (A) active  (B) act  (C) activate  (D) activity

28

4. 動詞：Anyone who ------- more than 100 dollars for the rebuilding of the theater can attend a preview screening.
   (A) donates   (B) donors   (C) donators   (D) donations

5. 動詞：The cafeteria ------- healthy meals and beverages high in fiber and low in calories, along with a lot of fresh fruit and vegetables.
   (A) serves   (B) servers   (C) services   (D) servants

6. 動詞：Some experts severely ------- the movie released the other day as boring and dull.
   (A) critic   (B) critical   (C) criticism   (D) criticized

7. 形容詞：The restaurant, where we had the farewell party for Mr. Lee, offers excellent Italian cuisine and desserts at ------- prices.
   (A) reason   (B) resonance   (C) reasonable   (D) reasonless

8. 形容詞：The comments the critic wrote about his performance are ------- and to the point.
   (A) appropriate   (B) approximate   (C) accurately   (D) adequately

9. 副詞：The bar I happened to go into the other day had a ------- warm and casual atmosphere.
   (A) realistic   (B) really   (C) realize   (D) reality

10. 副詞：A small fire broke out in the museum, but ------- the exhibits were not damaged.
    (A) happiness   (B) good luck   (C) lucky   (D) fortunately

---

### 解法のポイント　　接尾辞に注目して品詞を見分ける

まずは品詞の機能を学ぼう。名詞は主語・目的語・補語になる。形容詞は名詞を修飾したり、補語になったりする。副詞は動詞・形容詞・副詞、さらには文全体を修飾する。品詞の機能が分かってきたら、次に大事なのが品詞を見分けることだ。接尾辞などに注目して、品詞を見分けられるようになろう。

# Part 7  スキャニングをマスターしよう

スキャニング（scanning）とは、必要な情報を探し出して文書を読む方法で、この方法をマスターすると、TOEICの長文問題を素早く解くことが可能になる。先に質問に目を通して必要な情報のターゲットを絞り、それがどこにあるか、目をサーチライトのようにして探してみよう。

**Questions 1-4** refer to the following menu.

---

### SAMMY'S KITCHEN

Mon.-Fri.: Lunch 11:00 a.m.-3:00 p.m.   Dinner 6:00 p.m.-9:00 p.m.
Sat. & Sun.: Lunch 10:00 a.m.-2:00 p.m.   Dinner 5:00 p.m.-9:00 p.m.

#### SANDWICHES
**Available All Day**
**Cheese add-ons (All $2.00):** Mozzarella Cheese, Goat Cheese, Cheddar Cheese
**Meat add-ons:** Roast Beef $2.75, Turkey $2.75, Prosciutto $3.50
**Vegetable add-ons:** Tomatoes $1.00, Onions $1.25, Roasted Peppers $2.25

**LUCY'S SANDWICH**
 1/2 lb fresh ground beef with grilled onions and juicy bacon   $7.25
**JEFF'S SANDWICH**
 Grilled boneless breast chicken marinated with our original sauce and home-made coleslaw   $7.25
**AUNTIE'S SANDWICH**
 Smoked salmon, tomato, chopped onions, lettuce, and crispy bacon with our original yogurt sauce   $6.25
**JONATHAN'S SANDWICH**
 Barbecued tofu, cherry tomatoes, thinly sliced red onions, and fresh corn kernels   $5.25

#### SIDES

French Fries   $3.50    Onion Rings   $3.50    Caesar Salad   $3.95
\* All sides are available for $1.00 during lunch time on weekdays.

#### SOUPS

Chicken & Veggie   $4.00    Creamy Mushroom   $4.25

1. Which sandwich does NOT have onions?
   (A) Lucy's Sandwich
   (B) Jeff's Sandwich
   (C) Auntie's Sandwich
   (D) Jonathan's Sandwich

2. Which sandwich does NOT have meat?
   (A) Lucy's Sandwich
   (B) Jeff's Sandwich
   (C) Auntie's Sandwich
   (D) Jonathan's Sandwich

3. When can people NOT eat at Sammy's Kitchen?
   (A) At noon every day
   (B) At 5:00 p.m. on Saturday
   (C) At 3:00 p.m. on Sunday
   (D) At 11:00 a.m. on Thursday

4. How much will it be if you order French fries and Lucy's Sandwich with added mozzarella cheese for lunch on Monday?
   (A) $7.25
   (B) $9.25
   (C) $10.25
   (D) $12.75

---

**解法のポイント**　　いきなり文章を読もうとしてはダメ

Part 7はとにかく分量が多いので、「①本文の上の枠外にある導入文→②本文のタイトルや1行目→③質問→④本文」の順番に目を通して、要領よく解き進めよう。①②に先に目を通しておくと、これから読む文章の形式や目的が分かるので、文章にすんなり入ることができる。また、③を見ておくと、全ての質問に答えてしまった時点で文章を読むのをやめることができるので、時間を短縮することができる。

# Unit 3 Cooking & Purchasing

名詞・主語と動詞の一致

## Part 1　ターゲット　　人物の「動作」に注目しよう

写真に人物が写っている場合、写真の人物がどういった場所や状況にいるのかだけでなく、その人物の性別や服装、特にその人物の「動作」に注目しよう。

Listen and fill in the blanks for each sentence. Then choose the statement that best describes what you see in the picture.

1.  　　　　　　　　　　　　　　　　　DL 14　　CD1-44 ～　CD1-48

(A) The man is cooking (　　　　)
　　(　　　) (　　　　　).
(B) The woman is (　　　　　)
　　(　　　　) (　　　　) their breakfast.
(C) The woman is (　　　　　) a
　　(　　　) (　　　　　) water.
(D) The man is taking a towel (　　　　)
　　(　　　) a (　　　　　).

Choose the statement that best describes what you see in the picture.

2.　　　　　　　　　　　　　　　　　CheckLink　　DL 15　　CD1-49

(A)　(B)　(C)　(D)

### 解法のポイント　　複数の人物が映っている写真は要注意

2人の人物が写っている問題では、はじめに読まれる主語に集中し、どちらか一方の人物の動作を述べているのか、あるいは両方の人物の動作について述べているのかを正確に聞き取ろう。また、2人の人物が同じ動作をしているのか、異なる動作をしているのかもよく見ること。音声と写真の両方を正確に処理できなければ、紛らわしい選択肢に引っかけられてしまう。

32

# Part 4　客に向けたアナウンスに慣れよう

店内放送やテレビショッピングなどの客向けのアナウンスは、「客への呼びかけ→注目商品の紹介→お得なセール期間→購入のススメ」という順番で展開することが多い。この展開を頭に入れつつ、質問を先読みして、聞き取らなければならない情報を限定しておけば、全部聞き取ろうとして焦らなくても済む。

Listen to the short talk and fill in the blanks. Then choose the best answer to each question.

Thank you for watching Shop Now TV! Today we have this beautiful (1.　　　　) (2.　　　　) from Harry's. Harry's is a well-known leather (3.　　　　　　　) in England, and we (4.　　　　　　　) the (5.　　　　) of their items. This bag's (6.　　　　) is very sophisticated as you can see. And this bag has an accordion-like interior with three zippered (7.　　　　　　　) and it (8.　　　　) (9.　　　　) a detachable shoulder (10.　　　　), which is (11.　　　　　　　), like this. At stores you'd pay over $ (12.　　　　) for one, but today we (13.　　　　) them to you, our TV viewers, for only $ (14.　　　). Can you (15.　　　　) it? We also managed to (16.　　　　) the (17.　　　　　　　) and (18.　　　　　　　) costs this time. This special is valid only today on Shop Now TV. Call us (19.　　　　) (20.　　　　) at 1-800-SHOPNOW.

1. What is Harry's?
   (A) A TV shopping program
   (B) A leather goods company
   (C) A musical instruments company
   (D) The name of the item on sale

2. What is mentioned about the item?
   (A) It has an outside pocket.
   (B) There are three color choices.
   (C) You can adjust the strap.
   (D) The special price is only for the weekend.

3. How can people get the item at a discount?
   (A) Through an on-line shopping site　(C) By visiting Harry's
   (B) By calling Harry's　　　　　　　　(D) By calling a toll-free number

Listen to the short talk and choose the best answer to each question.

CheckLink　DL 18, 19　CD1-55 ~ CD1-58　CD1-59

**4.** Where is this announcement being made?
  (A) At a grocery store　　(C) At a restaurant
  (B) At an electronics store　(D) At a kitchen goods store

**5.** What day is today?
  (A) Monday　(B) Tuesday　(C) Saturday　(D) Sunday

**6.** Which is more than 50% off of the regular price?
  (A) Chicken drumsticks　(C) Milk
  (B) Ground beef　　　　(D) Chicken salad sandwiches

◆解法のポイント　　商品の特徴だけでなく、購入方法にも注意

Part 4には、What is mentioned about ~? という質問が入っていることが多い。店内放送やテレビショッピングなどの問題では、商品の特徴が具体的に述べられるため、そこに注意が向きがちだが、注文受付期間・購入方法・条件などが選択肢に入っている場合もあるので、後半も聞き落さないようにしよう。

# Part 5　ターゲット　名詞と、主語と動詞の呼応関係をマスターしよう

Choose the best answer to complete the sentence.　CheckLink

**1.** 不可算名詞：Sarah has a cup of coffee, ------- bread with butter and a boiled egg for breakfast every morning.
  (A) two slices of　(B) several　(C) three　(D) a small number of

**2.** 不可算名詞：My mother gave me ------- about buying appliances such as a microwave oven, a dishwasher and a refrigerator.
  (A) advise　(B) some advice　(C) few advice　(D) much advices

**3.** 不可算名詞：Since ------- I ordered had obvious defects, I called a toll-free number and inquired about how to have it returned or exchanged.
  (A) a few item　(B) much goods　(C) the merchandise　(D) their products

4. **紛らわしい名詞**：E-mail is prevalent as ------- of communication these days, but many people want notices, like bills or invoices, by conventional mail.
   (A) a means   (B) a mean   (C) something means   (D) some meanings

5. **紛らわしい名詞**：Our new kitchen is so small that it has ------- for a big cupboard where we can put all of our dishes and cutlery.
   (A) a room   (B) the rooms   (C) no room   (D) many rooms

6. **ほとんどの**：------- complaints we have been receiving from customers are about deliveries of fragile items.
   (A) Most of   (B) Every of the   (C) Almost   (D) Almost all the

7. **長い主語**：The number of complaints we receive from customers ------- nowadays.
   (A) increase   (B) were increased   (C) is increasing   (D) to increase

8. **長い主語**：The questionnaire they included in the package, along with the product, warranty and instructions ------- many typos.
   (A) have   (B) having   (C) haved   (D) has

9. **B as well as A**：If you purchase by the dozen, the handling cost, as well as the shipping cost, ------- free and we will give you up to a 20 % discount.
   (A) are   (B) is   (C) been   (D) am

10. **Both A and B**：If you purchase by the dozen, both the shipping cost and the handling cost ------- free and we will give you up to a 20% discount.
    (A) are   (B) is   (C) been   (D) am

---

◀ 解法のポイント　　　　まず不可算名詞を覚えよう　　　　➡➡➡

可算名詞・不可算名詞の区別は日本語にはない。英語の名詞を覚える際にはまず、可算名詞か不可算名詞かを確認するようにしよう。特に不可算名詞は、不定冠詞の a(n) や複数の (e)s が付かなかったり、a piece of などを付ける決まった数え方があったりして混乱しやすいので、まず不可算名詞をまとめて確認しよう。

# Part 7 ターゲット 広告・宣伝の形式に慣れよう

Part 7の長文問題では、広告や宣伝の問題は頻出パターンである。まず、誰が、どのような目的で、誰を対象に広告・宣伝をしているのかを把握しなければならない。

**Questions 1-4** refer to the following website.

## The Chelsea Kitchen

Located in the heart of Greenwich Village, The Chelsea Kitchen offers cooking classes to all food enthusiasts. The experienced chef and food expert, Barbara Rossi, teaches professional techniques and shares her most popular recipes in hands-on sessions. Barbara graduated from the California Culinary Academy in 1990 and worked in Paris and Rome for three years, respectively. After moving to New York in 1997, she worked at the world-famous restaurant, Il Giardino in Union Square, as their head chef. She is now the executive chef at Le Parc in Tribeca. She will open the doors of traditional French and Italian cooking through the flavors of the food and wine.

### Cooking Classes

Our cooking classes are small—a maximum of five students per class. All skill levels are welcome (no minors, please). Classes have a set price of $120, which includes fresh, organic ingredients, tools and supplies, and wine tasting with dinner. Bring a friend with you and get a discount. Register for classes together and you will each receive $10 off the fee.

### How to Register

To register online for a cooking class, check our class schedule and click "Register" on the class you wish to attend.

### Cancellation Policy

You can reschedule if we are notified at least 5 business days prior to the class you have signed up for. If you find you cannot make it to a class at the last minute, please consider finding someone to take your place. There are no refunds.

1. What kind of classes are provided at The Chelsea Kitchen?
   (A) How to use kitchen utensils
   (B) Cooking
   (C) Food education
   (D) How to grow organic vegetables

2. The word "hands-on" in paragraph 1, line 4, is closest in meaning to
   (A) practical
   (B) basic
   (C) fun
   (D) hard

3. How much is the total fee if you and a friend register for a class together?
   (A) $120
   (B) $220
   (C) $230
   (D) $240

4. What is NOT true about The Chelsea Kitchen?
   (A) Barbara Rossi has worked in Europe for six years.
   (B) The class is limited to a small number of participants.
   (C) You can register online for a class you'd like to attend.
   (D) You can get a refund if you cancel your registration 24 hours before a scheduled class.

---

**解法のポイント**　　　　見出しや導入文に注意

広告・宣伝文は、興味のない人にもインパクトを与えて目を引かなければならないため、見出しや導入文に、その広告・宣伝文の伝えたいメッセージが集約されていることが多い。ここに必ず目を通すようにしてから、詳細部分の読解の準備をしよう。

# Unit 4 Traffic & Travel

形容詞・副詞

## Part 1　ターゲット　人物が写っていない写真問題に慣れよう

Part 1の10問中、人物が全く写っていない写真の問題が1〜2問出題される。人物が写っていない風景写真タイプの問題に慣れよう。

Listen and fill in the blanks for each sentence. Then choose the statement that best describes what you see in the picture.

1.
DL 20　CD1-60 〜 CD1-64

(A) Some airplanes are (　　　　) in the (　　　) (　　　　　) on the ground.
(B) Some (　　　　　　) are (　　　　　　) the airplane.
(C) Some airplanes are (　　　　) (　　　) from a (　　　　) at the same time.
(D) Some (　　　　　) are (　　　　　) the trucks into the (　　　　).

Choose the statement that best describes what you see in the picture.

2.
DL 21　CD1-65

(A)　(B)　(C)　(D)

### 解法のポイント　写真全体を見る

人物が写っていない写真問題では、人物を描写する選択肢を候補から外せるため、選択肢を絞り込みやすいという利点がある一方で、写真の一部に意識を集中できないという難点もある。写真全体を広く見ながら、読まれたモノにすばやく反応して焦点を当て、写真と音声を比べるしかない。

# Part 2　ターゲット　　　WH 疑問文に慣れよう

WH 疑問文とは、what, when, where, who, which, why, whose, how などの疑問詞で始まる疑問文のことだ。これらの疑問詞は文の最初に読まれるので、聞き逃さないようにしなければならない。聞き逃してしまうと、選択肢がすべて聞き取れても正答を選べなくなってしまう。ただし、間接疑問文の場合は、疑問詞は文の途中にあるので要注意。

Listen and fill in the blanks for each sentence. Then choose the best response to each question or statement.

1. Why do you always take the (　　　　　) on the (　　　　)?
   (A) No, I don't have any (　　　　)(　　　　) me on the plane.
   (B) I can (　　　　)(　　　　)(　　　　) when I want to.
   (C) We had a good view of the (　　　)(　　　　)(　　　　) the plane window.

2. Would you (　　　　) to (　　　　)(　　　　) I can find the lost and found?
   (A) Next to the (　　　　)(　　　　) area.
   (B) It (　　　　)(　　　)(　　　　).
   (C) All (　　　　)(　　　　) are taken to the lost and found.

3. How many hours _____?
   (A) I take _____.
   (B) _____ an hour.
   (C) Yes, our company _____.

Listen to the question or statement and the three responses. Then choose the best response.

4. (A)　(B)　(C)

### 解法のポイント　　　Yes / No で答えている選択肢は除外

WH 疑問文に対して、Yes / No で始まる返答は不正解だと判断してよい。もちろん、日本語での会話と同じように、「場所」を尋ねる質問に対して、完璧な文ではなく「3 階で」「受付です」のように簡単な返答で済ませる場合もある。

# Part 6　形容詞と副詞の働きをマスターしよう

**Questions 1-4** refer to the following notice.

To: All Passengers

This is to inform you that Benton Station will begin making repairs and improvements to the aging -------, including the station plaza and the

    **1.** (A) plants
        (B) devices
        (C) facilities
        (D) locations

pavement around the station. This project is scheduled to take place for one year beginning from July 8 to the end of next June. Construction activities will be conducted from 8 a.m. to 8 p.m. Monday to Saturday.

During this period, the stores and restaurants in the area will be ------- through

    **2.** (A) accessible
        (B) accessibility
        (C) accessibly
        (D) access

temporary sidewalks, but vehicular traffic will be restricted around the station.

During the construction, the ticket gate and passenger access to the trains will change periodically. Please note the posted maps ------- the updated

    **3.** (A) show
        (B) showing
        (C) shown
        (D) be shown

construction site. We apologize for any inconvenience and thank you ------- for

    **4.** (A) later
        (B) in advance
        (C) however
        (D) afterward

your cooperation.

### 解法のポイント　　　英文の構造に注意

前後の文脈や文章全体を読まなくても、空所の前後を見るだけで解けるタイプの問題では、選択肢の単語の品詞を見抜くことと、空所に入る語の文中での働きを見抜くことが大切だ。特に頻出なのは、〈冠詞＋形容詞＋名詞〉と〈助動詞＋副詞＋動詞の原形〉のように単語と単語の間に「形容詞」や「副詞」が割り込んでくるタイプ。応用編として〈冠詞＋副詞＋形容詞＋名詞〉もある。

# Part 7　ターゲット　告知文書に慣れよう

イベントなどの告知文書には、「いつ」「誰が」「何を」「どこで」などの項目が記載されている。まずは最初の数10秒間で、そういった主要項目が文書のどこに書かれているかを把握しよう。そうすれば、質問の答えがどのあたりに書かれているか絞れるので、要領よく解答できる。

**Questions 1-4** refer to the following letter.

## BEST HIKING TRAVEL COMPANY

Thank you for choosing BEST HIKING TRAVEL COMPANY
Enjoy a beautiful tour of the Grande Pietra Mountains area!
Friday, October 7 – Saturday, October 8, 2016
$150 per person, single / $120 per person, twin / $100 per person, for 3-4 people

### HIKING ITINERARY

**Day 1**

| | |
|---|---|
| 8:30 AM | Meet at the bus terminal in front of the Grande Pietra City Hall. |
| 8:45 AM | Bus departs from the City Hall for the Grande Pietra Mountains Park. |
| 10:45 AM | Hiking on the Grande Pietra Mountains Park trails. Picnic lunch (please bring your own). |
| 1:00 PM | Exploring the 5-mile Lake Pietra Trail. This moderate trail leads you to an area offering incredible views of Lake Pietra. It is highly recommended that you take some pictures of the lake surrounded by maple trees with their leaves in full autumn colors. [*1] |
| 4:00 PM | Check into our hotel, the Grande Pietra Mountains Resort Hotel. [*2] |
| 5:00 PM | An all-you-can-eat poolside barbeque dinner at the hotel |

**Day 2**

| | |
|---|---|
| 7:00 AM | Breakfast at the hotel restaurant |
| 9:30 AM | Bus departs for the Grande Pietra Mountains Park. |
| 10:30 AM | Take the Waterfalls Trail. This trail leads you to wonderful views of Pietra River Falls, which is the highest waterfall in this state. [*3] |
| 12:00 PM | Lunch [*4] |
| 1:00 PM | Bus departs from the Park's parking lot for the City Hall. |

**NOTICE**
[*1] It is strongly recommended that you bring an outdoor jacket as it can get cold on the hiking trail.
[*2] The hotel receptionist will give you a meal voucher which can be used at the hotel restaurant for breakfast.
[*3] Visitors who have acrophobia or a fear of heights should not take this trail.
[*4] Be sure to purchase light meals or snacks at the shop in the hotel.

**Tour includes accommodations and meals except for two lunches.**
**Itinerary Subject to Change Due to Weather.**
**Payment Due by Thursday, August 4, 2016.**

1. Who is this document probably intended for?
   (A) A travel agent
   (B) A hotel manager
   (C) A tourist
   (D) A bus driver

2. What day is recommended for taking photos?
   (A) In the morning on October 7
   (B) In the afternoon on October 7
   (C) In the morning on October 8
   (D) In the evening on October 8

3. What is NOT included in the tour?
   (A) Friday dinner
   (B) Room charge for Friday
   (C) Lunch for two days
   (D) Saturday breakfast

4. Who is advised to refrain from visiting the waterfall?
   (A) People who are afraid of heights
   (B) People who do not want to get wet
   (C) People who do not have any cold weather outerwear
   (D) People who did not eat breakfast

・・・・・・・・・・・・・・・・・・・・・・・・・・・・・・・・・・・・・・・・・・・・・・・・・・・・・

解法のポイント　　　　注意事項を見逃さない　　　→ → →

主要項目の他に「注意事項」が文書末に記載されていることがある。この「注意事項」は文書内容の例外になるが、この部分に関する質問が出題されることが多い。Notice「注意」などの項目には必ず目を通すようにしよう。

Unit 4  Traffic & Travel  43

# Unit 5 Advertising & ICT

時制

## Part 1　ターゲット　　動詞の時制を聞き取ろう

Part 1では、写真に写っていること以外は正解ではない。したがって、過去時制や未来時制が含まれている選択肢は不正解である。

Listen and fill in the blanks for each sentence. Then choose the statement that best describes what you see in the picture.

1.　　　　　　　　　　　　　　CheckLink　DL 26　CD2-01 ～ CD2-05

(A) A sidewalk sign is (　　　　　) (　　　　　　　) in front of the store.
(B) There is an (　　　　　　　) (　　　　　　　　) hanging from a sunshade.
(C) Customers (　　　　) (　　　　　　) on the bench.
(D) Tables and chairs (　　　　) (　　　　) on the (　　　　　　) in front of the shop.

Choose the statement that best describes what you see in the picture.

2.　　　　　　　　　　　　　　CheckLink　DL 27　CD2-06

(A)　(B)　(C)　(D)

### 解法のポイント　弱く読まれる動詞や聞き間違いやすい動詞に注意

Part 1では、文頭の主語の聞き取りも大切だが、その次に来る動詞も正確に聞き取らなければならない。特に、be動詞や一般動詞（規則動詞）の過去形・過去分詞につけられる -ed は、軽く発音される場合が多いので注意が必要だ。また、進行形や受動態、完了形で使われる is と has、being と been は発音も似ているので、聞き間違えないようにしよう。

# Part 3  ターゲット　　質問と選択肢を先に読もう

会話が流れてくる前に、質問と選択肢を読むようにしたい。時間に余裕がない場合でも、せめて質問にだけは目を通して、聞き取らなければならない会話のポイントを逃さないようにすることが必要である。

Listen to the conversation and fill in the blanks. Then choose the best answer to each question.　　CheckLink　DL 28　CD2-07 ~ CD2-11

M: Did you get the (1.　　　　) from Meg? She told me she would send it as an (2.　　　　) (3.　　　　) a couple of days ago.

W: No, I didn't. I (4.　　　　) her computer is (5.　　　　) with a (6.　　　　), which makes her computer (7.　　　　) itself (8.　　　　). She must be in big (9.　　　　) now.

M: I'm in a (10.　　　　). I (11.　　　　) the document for next week's meeting.

W: Meg said she (12.　　　　) to (13.　　　　) her license for the antivirus (14.　　　　). Shall I call and (15.　　　　) her when her computer (16.　　　　) (17.　　　　) (18.　　　　)?

1. What is the man's problem?　　DL 29　CD2-12
   (A) The man cannot attach the file.
   (B) The man doesn't have the document.
   (C) The man will have to postpone the meeting until next week.
   (D) The man cannot install the antivirus software.

2. Why has Meg been having trouble with her computer?
   (A) Meg updated the antivirus software.
   (B) Meg sent the document as an attached file.
   (C) Meg renewed a software license.
   (D) Meg has got a virus on her computer.

3. What will the woman probably do next?
   (A) Telephone Meg about her computer
   (B) Send an e-mail to Meg
   (C) Fix Meg's computer
   (D) Delete the virus from Meg's computer

Unit 5　Advertising & ICT　45

Listen to the conversation and choose the best answer to each question.

CheckLink　　DL 30, 31　　CD2-13 ~ CD2-17　　CD2-18

**4.** What are the speakers mainly talking about?

(A) How to attract tourists

(B) How to go to Mexico

(C) Where to travel in summer

(D) Where to get brochures

**5.** When did the man go to Mexico?

(A) Yesterday　　(C) This summer

(B) Last summer　　(D) At the end of the year

**6.** What will the woman probably do next?

(A) Write an article about hotels in Mexico

(B) Consider her travel destination for this summer

(C) Visit a travel agency to get brochures

(D) Place an advertisement promoting Cancun on the Internet

---

**解法のポイント**　　**5W1H に注意**

Part 3の質問では、when「いつ」、where「どこで」、who「誰が」、what「何を」、why「なぜ」、how「どのように」したのか／するのか、といったことを問われる。全体の内容に加え、話し手が言及する具体的な曜日・時間や場所、数字にも注意しなければならない。

# Part 5　ターゲット　　時制をマスターしよう

---

Choose the best answer to complete the sentence.　　CheckLink

**1. 基本時制**：Last night I ------- my laptop which I had bought only 3 weeks ago and, sad to say, it broke.

(A) dropped　(B) have dropped　(C) would drop　(D) was dropping

**2. 状態動詞**：Henry ------- various gadgets, such as a smart phone, a tablet, and a portable music player.

(A) have　(B) haves　(C) has　(D) are having

3. 状態動詞：She still ------- an impressive TV commercial she saw when she was a child, about thirty years ago.
   (A) memory    (B) remembers    (C) is remembering    (D) had memorial

4. 副詞節：More people will enjoy e-commerce with no worries if information security and copyright issues -------.
   (A) solves    (B) will be solved    (C) has solved    (D) are solved

5. 名詞節：Our spokesperson is trying to stress the novelty of our new product, but its design is so bad that some of us doubt if it ------- well.
   (A) sells    (B) will sell    (C) has sold    (D) is sold

6. 進行形：Don't power off your computer while you ------- the patch.
   (A) to download and install    (C) are downloading and installing
   (B) downloading or installed    (D) will be downloaded or installed

7. 完了形：As Maggie ------- her antivirus software, her computer can get infected with a virus at any time.
   (A) have not updated    (C) not had updated
   (B) has never updated    (D) never haved updated

8. 完了形：They ------- the launch of a promotion campaign for their new multifunctional printer by next Friday.
   (A) will have announced    (C) will be announced
   (B) will be announcing    (D) will have to be announcing

9. 完了進行形：The TV station ------- news programs every morning, noon and evening since 1995.
   (A) had been on air    (C) has been broadcasting
   (B) have been aired    (D) will have broadcasted

10. 完了進行形：The brochure which he ------- hard on for two months looked neither well-designed nor attractive.
    (A) worked    (C) has been working
    (B) had worked    (D) had been working

**解法のポイント**　時制問題は時間軸をイメージして

日本語は時制があいまいなので、英語の完了形と過去形、完了進行形と進行形を区別するのが苦手な人は多い。和訳に頼ると混乱しやすいので、常に時間軸をイメージして問題を解くようにしよう。

# Part 7　ターゲット　スキミングをマスターしよう

スキミング（skimming）とは、文章の要点を文字通り「すくい取る（skim）」ことである。質問の第1問目では文章の概要について出題されることが多いので、文章の要点は何かということを必ず意識しながら読み進めていこう。

**Questions 1-4** refer to the following notice.

## Bulletin

This is an announcement for all employees of the sales department.

　Effective immediately, this company is launching a promotion campaign to coincide with the release of the new line of smartphones from Pony. We are losing customers to our competitors. We need to increase the sign-up rate and slow the rate of people switching from our company. A new series of commercials will be broadcast on TV channels nationwide. New brochures will highlight the following points that make our services more attractive to customers.

- Unlimited access to the Internet for less than $100 per month.
- Browse the Internet using the most user-friendly browser without worrying about any surprise fees.
- The newest smartphone has the eagerly awaited e-commerce function which allows payments to be made directly from the phone.
- Updating personal information and renewing the service contract can be done completely online, eliminating the need to visit the nearest shop.
- We recognize that information security is of utmost importance. We maintain the newest and best software to deal with spam and viruses, and regularly provide patches to ensure the safety of customer's information on their gadget.

　To make this an effective promotion campaign we would like you to focus on these points when promoting our products and services to customers. Let's make this the best campaign we've ever had, and get back on the winning track. Thank you for your cooperation.

1. What does this bulletin give information about?
   (A) A new phone
   (B) The sales department
   (C) A promotion campaign
   (D) New customers

2. Where will the new commercials be broadcast?
   (A) On local TV
   (B) On national TV
   (C) On new brochures
   (D) On the Internet

3. Which of these prices is likely for unlimited Internet access per month?
   (A) For free
   (B) $90
   (C) $100
   (D) $110

4. What should salespeople focus on when promoting the products and services?
   (A) Unlimited Internet access
   (B) The e-commerce function
   (C) High quality information security
   (D) All of the above

---

### 解法のポイント　　質問の順番に出てくるヒント

通常、ピンポイントで解答を探すことができるタイプの問題は、質問の順番に沿って本文中にヒントが現れる。質問の番号によって、あらかじめ本文のどのあたりに解答のヒントがあるのか目星をつけながら読むことができるはずだ。

# Unit 6  Production & Logistics

接続詞・前置詞

## Part 1　ターゲット　　類義語や言い換えに注意しよう

写真を描写する際、単純な単語や表現を避けて、あえて難しい表現で言い換えていることがよくある。先入観を捨て写真を素直に見て、最後まで音声を聞いてから選択しよう。

Listen and fill in the blanks for each sentence. Then choose the statement that best describes what you see in the picture.

1.　　　　DL 32　CD2-19 ~ CD2-23

(A) Workers are (　　　　　) the airplane with some (　　　　　).
(B) Ground (　　　) is (　　　　　) (　　　　　) cargo from an airplane.
(C) A vehicle is (　　　　　) the (　　　　　).
(D) Air cargo transporters (　　　) (　　　　　) in a line.

Choose the statement that best describes what you see in the picture.

2.　　　CheckLink　DL 33　CD2-24

(A)　(B)　(C)　(D)

### 解法のポイント　　自分の語彙に縛られない

例えば、写真に自動車が写っているとする。それを見た瞬間に car という語を思い浮かべるかもしれないが、選択肢では car ではなく automobile や vehicle と表現されているかもしれない。日ごろから、類義語辞典や英英辞典を活用して、こまめに類義語を確認してほしい。

# Part 4 ターゲット 「誰に向かって話しているのか」をつかもう

Part 4では、「話し手は誰か」を問う問題だけでなく、それを逆にした「聞き手は誰か」を問う問題も出題される。"Attention, passengers" などの、話し手から聞き手への呼びかけですぐに「聞き手」が誰か分かる場合もあれば、場面や状況を特定して初めて、「聞き手」が分かる場合もある。

Listen to the short talk and fill in the blanks. Then choose the best answer to each question.

(1.          ) (2.          ) Whole Natural Industries. My name is Sharon Snider, and I'll be your (3.          ) for the next two hours. Let me (4.          ) with a short (5.          ) of Whole Natural Industries. We are one of the (6.          ) (7.          ) companies in the industry. Our products are (8.          ) (9.          ) (10.          ) the (11.          ) and have a great reputation because of our efforts to use as many (12.          ) (13.          ) as possible. Many snack foods contain (14.          ) additives and preservatives, something we make a strong effort not to use. If you are (15.          ) (16.          ) our snacks, I will (17.          ) about the (18.          ) we offer on (19.          ) (20.          ) after the (21.          ) (22.          ), but first, we'll go outside to see how we grow (23.          ) and (24.          ) organically.

1. Where is this talk taking place?
   (A) At an amusement park    (C) At a farm
   (B) At a snack company      (D) On a TV program

2. What is mentioned about Whole Natural Industries?
   (A) They are the oldest snack company in this country.
   (B) They are using only organic ingredients.
   (C) They offer discounts on regular purchases.
   (D) They have a tour every month.

3. What will the group probably do next?
   (A) Go outside the building
   (B) See how they make snacks
   (C) Ask questions about a yearly contract
   (D) Pick up fruit at the company's farm

Unit 6 Production & Logistics

Listen to the short talk and choose the best answer to each question.

**4.** Who is the speaker addressing?
   (A) A rescue party
   (B) Customers
   (C) Radio news audience
   (D) Sales staff

**5.** What is the problem?
   (A) A new line of cars is not selling well.
   (B) A typhoon hit the speaker's office.
   (C) They cannot sell their new line of cars as they planned.
   (D) They cannot contact the factory in Thailand.

**6.** When will the company probably start shipping their new products?
   (A) In September        (C) In November
   (B) In October          (D) In December

**解法のポイント　ツアーガイドの話は、特に最初と最後に集中する**

Part 4では「ツアーガイド」の話が頻出するが、観光地を巡る旅行ガイドだけでなく、会社や工場、美術館や水族館などの内部見学ツアーの案内役が話し手になることもよくある。いずれにせよ、最初に述べられる自己紹介と、最後の方に述べられるツアー特典、集合場所・時間、今後の行き先などが、解答のカギを握っている。

# Part 5　ターゲット　接続詞と前置詞をマスターしよう

Choose the best answer to complete the sentence.

**1.** 接続詞：------- we unload cargos at the dock, we sort them in the warehouse and get them ready for shipping.
   (A) As far as   (B) As good as   (C) As well as   (D) As soon as

**2.** 接続詞：------- you handle hazardous materials or explosives carefully, you can cause a serious accident.
   (A) Unless   (B) Until   (C) Because   (D) Once

3. **前置詞**：These containers are carried from a manufacturer to a wholesaler ------- freight train.
   (A) with  (B) by their  (C) in the  (D) by

4. **前置詞**：Our garage makes it a rule to have our industrial waste collected ------- the morning of the first Tuesday of every month.
   (A) on  (B) in  (C) at  (D) to

5. **群前置詞**：According to the newspaper, an explosion which took place at the chemical plant yesterday was ------- poor maintenance of their facility.
   (A) up to  (B) due to  (C) in addition to  (D) with regard to

6. **群前置詞**：The top automaker decided to update its assembly line with new equipment ------- increasing productivity and safety.
   (A) in touch with      (C) with a view to
   (B) in the place of    (D) within reach of

7. **接続詞と前置詞**：------- this product is made of highly durable materials, it is not heat-resistant.
   (A) Instead of  (B) In spite of  (C) Though  (D) However

8. **接続詞と前置詞**：They experimented ------- thousands of hours to make special artificial silk, and they finally succeeded and applied for a patent.
   (A) while  (B) among  (C) during  (D) for

9. **接続詞と前置詞**：------- the architect who designed the building was inspecting the construction site, he found a serious error in his design.
   (A) While  (B) Among  (C) During  (D) For

10. **接続詞と前置詞**：They patiently continued to make more than 50 models ------- they completed a prototype.
    (A) by  (B) up to  (C) until  (D) after

---

**◀解法のポイント　　和訳や意味の似ている接続詞と前置詞に注意　➡➡➡**

前置詞 during, for, among や接続詞 while は使い方や意味が異なるが、すべて「あいだ」と和訳されてしまう。また、前置詞 by、接続詞 by the time、前置詞・接続詞 until [till] もすべて「～まで」と和訳されてしまう。このように紛らわしい接続詞と前置詞は、品詞と意味に気をつけて、正確に使い分けられるようになろう。

Unit 6  Production & Logistics ○ 53

# Part 7 ターゲット　記事に慣れよう

新聞やウェブサイトの記事は、出だしが勝負。見出しを読んで、どんな内容か大まかに推測できれば、続く本文の内容が理解しやすい。また、最初の数行、あるいは第１パラグラフには、全体の内容が集約されているので、気をつけて読みたい。見出しのそばに小さく掲載されている、本文が書かれた日付や発行日に関連する質問が出ることもある。

**Questions 1-4** refer to the following article.

## Naturalife Forms a Strategic Business Alliance with CREA Next Spring
**September 30, 2015**

　Naturalife, one of the big household goods and furniture retailers, has announced that they will go into partnership with CREA. The president of Naturalife, Amy Douglas, said, "The partnership will help our company strengthen and diversify our business, and enhance our potential for growth in the home furnishings marketplace."

　Beginning in 1911 as a small retailer, Naturalife has grown into a large chain selling home furnishings in contemporary designs, and now has 100 stores in 12 countries. CREA started as a furniture retailer in 1985, and has increased its earnings at a terrific rate, with at least five new locations opening every year. The driving force behind this growth is their "do-it-yourself" style.

　The partnership should be finalized in half a year. Introducing the strategy of CREA, Naturalife will be able to develop a more efficient logistics system and generate innovative designs. CREA will continue to be a separate brand, with its own products and management.

1. The word "enhance" in paragraph 1, line 5, is closest in meaning to
   (A) negotiate
   (B) inspect
   (C) suspend
   (D) improve

2. How can CREA be described?
   (A) Failing
   (B) Expanding
   (C) Stagnant
   (D) Shrinking

3. What is implied from this article?
   (A) Naturalife and CREA will open at least five new locations every year.
   (B) Customers can ask staff at a service counter of CREA to assemble furniture.
   (C) The new target of Naturalife and CREA is ecologically-minded people.
   (D) CREA will not undergo a merger with Naturalife.

4. When will the partnership be finalized?
   (A) December, 2015
   (B) January, 2016
   (C) March, 2016
   (D) September, 2016

---

**解法のポイント　　　語彙力増強で短時間に解答　→→→**

Part 7では、文中の単語の意味を問われることがある。文脈から判断する方法もあるが、単語の意味を知っていれば、長い文を読まずに正解を選ぶこともできる。ただし、複数の意味を持つ単語の場合、早合点しないよう気をつけなければならない。語彙力増強には地道な努力が必要。

# Review Test 1

## Part 1

 CheckLink  CD2-35

Look at the picture and choose the statement that best describes what you see in the picture.

**1.**

(A)  (B)  (C)  (D)

**2.**

(A)  (B)  (C)  (D)

56

3.

(A)   (B)   (C)   (D)

4.

(A)   (B)   (C)   (D)

## Part 2

CheckLink   CD2-36

Listen to the question or statement and the three responses. Then choose the best response to each question or statement.

5. Mark your answer on your answer sheet.   (A)   (B)   (C)
6. Mark your answer on your answer sheet.   (A)   (B)   (C)
7. Mark your answer on your answer sheet.   (A)   (B)   (C)
8. Mark your answer on your answer sheet.   (A)   (B)   (C)
9. Mark your answer on your answer sheet.   (A)   (B)   (C)
10. Mark your answer on your answer sheet.   (A)   (B)   (C)

# Part 3

Listen to the conversations and choose the best answer to each question.

**11.** Where is the conversation taking place?
   (A) In a room    (B) In a hotel    (C) In a train    (D) In an airplane

**12.** When will the woman come back?
   (A) In the morning
   (B) In the afternoon
   (C) In the evening
   (D) Not mentioned

**13.** What does the man ask the woman to do when she returns?
   (A) Give the key to the man
   (B) Keep the valuables in the safe
   (C) Check the woman's money
   (D) Show the ticket

---

**14.** What are the speakers discussing?
   (A) Renovation of the laboratory
   (B) Change of the color of the walls in the lavatory
   (C) Failure of the experiment
   (D) Visit to the laboratory chief's house

**15.** What is the man worried about?
   (A) Maintenance of the machines
   (B) Interruption of the work
   (C) Work noise
   (D) Office relocation

**16.** According to the woman, how long will it take for the work to be completed?
   (A) About a week
   (B) About half a month
   (C) About a month
   (D) About two months

# Part 4

Listen to the short talks and choose the best answer to each question.

**17.** What made the flight delayed?
   (A) Snow storm in Boston
   (B) Late arrival of the airplane
   (C) A sick passenger
   (D) Engine trouble

**18.** When will the flight take off?
   (A) At 11:15 p.m.   (B) At 11:40 a.m.   (C) At midnight   (D) At noon

**19.** What should passengers do if they have questions about the flight?
   (A) Send an e-mail to customer services
   (B) Go to the airline service counter
   (C) Make a phone call to Blue Sky Airlines
   (D) Go to the departure gate

---

**20.** Where is Randall Spa?
   (A) At the top of a mountain
   (B) In the city center
   (C) By a lake
   (D) In a suburb

**21.** What is the speaker's recommendation?
   (A) Aroma steam rooms
   (B) An indoor bath
   (C) A rooftop bath
   (D) Hot stone therapies

**22.** What must you do to eat at the restaurant next to the spa?
   (A) Pay 38 dollars in advance
   (B) Buy a four-hour ticket
   (C) Show your spa ticket and pay an additional five dollars
   (D) Make a reservation in advance

# Part 5

Choose the best answer to complete the sentence.

**23.** In recent years, nursing facilities have ------- it more difficult to secure adequate care worker human resources.
(A) knew   (B) understood   (C) found   (D) founded

**24.** None of the cast nor the film director present at the film premiere would ------- any reason for the leading actor's absence.
(A) registration   (B) attraction   (C) accommodation   (D) mention

**25.** Subways are always crowded in the morning rush hour, so we should try to make ------- for one another.
(A) room   (B) a room   (C) rooms   (D) roomy

**26.** Neither Mr. O'Donnell nor his colleague ------- checked in yet because their flight was delayed and they missed their connecting flight.
(A) has   (B) is   (C) have   (D) are

**27.** Marissa has ------- skin, so she always tries to choose mild and natural detergents and avoids synthetic textiles.
(A) sense   (B) sensible   (C) sensitive   (D) sensual

**28.** This decaf coffee ------- safe and natural ingredients; it is rich in vitamins and minerals.
(A) contaminant   (B) contains   (C) is containing   (D) container

**29.** When you ------- to the digital edition of this magazine, a message with your ID and password will be sent to your e-mail address.
(A) subscription   (B) subscribe   (C) will subscribe   (D) subscript

**30.** Once the main approach and parking lot ------- with blocks, construction vehicles won't be allowed to enter the site.
(A) pave   (B) will pave   (C) are paved   (D) will be paving

**31.** Despite ------- for a publisher over the past three years since graduating from university, Emily decided to go to graduate school to get an MA.
(A) worked   (B) having worked   (C) will work   (D) to work

**32.** ------- this timetable, the flight bound for San Francisco via Hong Kong will arrive at its destination at 5:30 p.m. local time.
(A) In addition to   (B) Due to   (C) Contrary to   (D) According to

# Part 6

**Questions 33-36** refer to the following advertisement.

## FOR PERSONAL AND BUSINESS STORAGE

Looking for extra space? Having trouble keeping sensitive business documents? LOCKERS, Self-Storage Service, is committed to -------

**33.** (A) provide
(B) provided
(C) providing
(D) be provided

customers with a number of solutions for all types of storage needs at affordable rates.

All our facilities are equipped with state-of-the-art security systems such as individual door alarms and around-the-clock surveillance and are available to access anytime you like with your PIN code. In addition, all our units are climate-controlled. Self-storage units vary in size from ministorage units for children's toys to larger units that can ------- bikes, RVs and boats. -------, our

**34.** (A) designate
(B) fascinate
(C) collaborate
(D) accommodate

**35.** (A) Plus
(B) Rather
(C) In contrast
(D) Initially

specially trained staff members are available on a 24-hour basis.

To celebrate our fifth anniversary, we're pleased to offer you this special discount: no security deposit and one month free rent! This special offer will be good ------- the end of March.

**36.** (A) while
(B) by
(C) during
(D) until

Call us at 0800 111 2525 or stop by our facilities today, so one of our friendly managers can find the perfect unit for you!

# Part 7

**Questions 37-40** refer to the following website and review.

---

**Magazine Subscription**                                      🛒 $0.00 (0 items)

| All Categories | Best Sellers | Men's | Women's | Teen's | Children's | Search by Magazine or Keyword |

## *Beauté Monthly*

About Beauté Monthly

First published in 1950, the magazine focuses on the latest fashion, cosmetics, health, and entertainment news. Beauté, which means "beauty" in French, features not only fashion and beauty tips but also articles on women's lifestyles and social issues across the globe.

Women interested in fashion, beauty, and modern feminine lifestyles would enjoy a subscription to Beauté Monthly!

## *Monthly Print Magazine Subscription*

| | | |
|---|---|---|
| 8 issues | Newsstand: $31.92<br>price **$7.97 (You Save 75%)** | Add to Cart ▷▷ |
| 12 issues | Newsstand: $47.88<br>price **$10.00 (You Save 79%)** | Add to Cart ▷▷ |
| 24 issues | Newsstand: $95.76<br>price **$16.00 (You Save 83%)** | Add to Cart ▷▷ |

If you are not 100% satisfied with your magazine subscription, you will receive a 100% refund for all undelivered issues, at any time, for any reason.

---

▶▶▶ **Most-Liked Positive Review**

**I look forward to every issue.**

I used to subscribe to Beauté Monthly when I was in college. I came back because this site offered a good deal. I was pleasantly surprised at how Beauté Monthly has changed with the times. The health and beauty tips are very informative and the makeup, clothing, hair, jewelry, and perfume ads are fabulous! I also enjoy interesting articles concerning relationships, friendships, family, and women's issues.

**37.** What is the purpose of this website?
   (A) To persuade people to buy this magazine at a newsstand
   (B) To explain how to read this magazine both in print and online
   (C) To introduce this magazine to fashion editors
   (D) To encourage people to subscribe to the magazine

**38.** How much is a one-year subscription to this magazine?
   (A) $7.97
   (B) $10.00
   (C) $16.00
   (D) $79.00

**39.** What is indicated about subscribing to this magazine?
   (A) This magazine has been published since the 19th century.
   (B) You can get a 79% discount if you subscribe to this magazine for 2 years.
   (C) You should click the Add to Cart button if you want to read this magazine online.
   (D) You can cancel your subscription and get a refund for any issues you have not yet received.

**40.** What is true about the reviewer?
   (A) The reviewer is not satisfied with the subscription fee.
   (B) The reviewer thinks the magazine has too many fashion and beauty ads.
   (C) The reviewer had stopped subscribing to the magazine, but started again.
   (D) The reviewer is not interested in reading articles.

# Unit 7　Business & Economics

助動詞

## Part 1　ターゲット　　人や物の位置関係を正確にとらえよう

これまでの章で、①写真に写っている人や物を表す名詞に安易に飛びつかない、②動詞まで確認する、とアドバイスしてきた。この2つが安定してできるようになってきたら、次は人や物の位置関係まで聞き取ることを目指そう。

Listen and fill in the blanks for each sentence. Then choose the statement that best describes what you see in the picture.

1. 　　DL 38　　CD2-41 ～ CD2-45

(A) People are standing (　　　　) (　　　　) each other (　　　　) the desk.
(B) Some people are printing the handouts (　　　) (　　　) (　　　).
(C) People are reading the (　　　　　) documents (　　　　) the wall.
(D) Some people are putting their (　　　　) (　　　　) the desk.

Choose the statement that best describes what you see in the picture.

2. 　　CheckLink　　DL 39　　CD2-46

(A)　(B)　(C)　(D)

### 解法のポイント　　動作とその対象物の関係に注意

主語と動詞までは正確に写真を描写した英文であったとしても、動作の対象（＝目的語）や場所が異なっていれば、当然不正解である。「誰が・どうしている」の先の、「何を・どこで」というポイントまで聞き取る練習をしてほしい。

# Part 2　ターゲット　質問ではない疑問文に慣れよう

Part 2では、尋ねられた質問に適切に答えるというのが基本形だが、中には形式は疑問文だが、内容が単なる「質問」ではなく、実際には「提案」や「依頼」になっているタイプもあるので要注意。

Listen and fill in the blanks for each sentence. Then choose the best response to each question or statement.　CheckLink　DL 40〜42　CD2-47

CD2-48 〜 CD2-51

1. What (　　　) I (　　) you?
   (A) I'll (　　) you my (　　　　) (　　　　).
   (B) I (　　　) like you (　　　) (　　　) me Andy.
   (C) I (　　　) the client to (　　　　) the budget.

   CD2-52 〜 CD2-55

2. You (　　　　　) a report about the (　　　　) (　　　　) to the boss, didn't you?
   (A) No, I haven't (　　　　) (　　　) yet.
   (B) Yes, I've just (　　　　　) the (　　　　) of the mountain.
   (C) Yes, (　　　) (　　　) fine.

   CD2-56 〜 CD2-59

3. _____ our market share?
   (A) I'm planning _____.
   (B) Sure, I'll try and _____.
   (C) He will be _____ division.

Listen to the question or statement and the three responses. Then choose the best response.

4. (A)　(B)　(C)　CheckLink　DL 43　CD2-60

### 解法のポイント　パターンを暗記するのが近道

「質問ではない疑問文」のうち、Will[Would] you 〜 ? や Can[Could] you 〜 ? などの「〜してくれませんか」という依頼文に「いいですよ」の意味で返す場合、Certainly, Sure, Of course, OK, No problem などの定型句で返すのが普通なので、そのまま暗記した方が断然早い。ただし、Do you mind -ing? に「いいですよ」の意味で返す場合は、No, not at all などの否定の定型句で応じるので気をつけよう。

Unit 7　Business & Economics　65

# Part 5　助動詞をマスターしよう

**Choose the best answer to complete the sentence.**

1. 助動詞の用法：We have been boosting sales steadily, so if we can carry on this way, in a decade our company ------- one of the leading companies.
   - (A) will become
   - (B) will becomes
   - (C) will became
   - (D) will becoming

2. 助動詞の意味：Anyone ------- consult a consumer center or use a cooling-off period even after he or she has signed a contract.
   - (A) won't
   - (B) can
   - (C) would often
   - (D) can't help

3. 助動詞の意味：Although our competitor has an advantage over us, we ------- compromise easily in the merger negotiations.
   - (A) should
   - (B) must not
   - (C) are able to
   - (D) ought to

4. 助動詞＋助動詞：Exchange rates have been unstable recently, and we ------- keep a close eye on their future course for the next few weeks.
   - (A) will must
   - (B) must will
   - (C) will have to
   - (D) must be going to

5. 助動詞＋助動詞：Angela is so competent and energetic that she ------- develop a new market and get potential customers for it.
   - (A) can must
   - (B) must can
   - (C) can have to
   - (D) must be able to

6. 助動詞＋過去の表現：As his firm has been prosperous despite the depression, he ------- bankrupt.
   - (A) cannot went
   - (B) cannot have gone
   - (C) can was going
   - (D) can had been going

**7.** ～しなくてもよい：Their explanation was obviously insufficient and it's their fault, so you ------- pay an additional fee.
(A) can
(B) may well
(C) don't have to
(D) haven't to

**8.** ～しない方がよい：It's true that Douglas is a successful entrepreneur in various ventures, but he often talks big, so you ------- accept blindly what he says.
(A) didn't have better
(B) not had better
(C) had not better
(D) had better not

**9.** ～しないために：The Government must take effective measures to stimulate the economy so that it ------- deteriorate further.
(A) won't
(B) want
(C) mustn't
(D) shouldn't

**10.** 仮定法現在：On the basis of his analysis that the stock market will go up thanks to deregulation, he recommended that his clients ------- some stocks at once.
(A) purchase
(B) purchased
(C) had purchased
(D) be purchased

---

◀解法のポイント▶　　助動詞のイメージをしっかり確認しよう　→→→

助動詞は、動詞の前に付けて動詞に「意志・可能・義務」などの意味を添えたり、「～だろう、～かもしれない、～に違いない」など、話し手の確信の度合いを表したりする品詞で、それぞれ基本イメージをもっている。そのイメージと使い分けを正確に確認しながら勉強した方が、混乱しにくく、効率的だ。

# Part 7 ターゲット　手紙やメールに慣れよう

TOEICの場合、手紙やメールはビジネス関連の内容で、①今までの両者の関係について述べた「挨拶」→②今回の手紙・メールの目的について述べた「本題」→③今後の展望や展開について述べた「まとめ、追伸」の順に展開する。このパターン化した3段階の展開に慣れよう。

**Questions 1-4** refer to the following e-mail.

| To: | Lawrence Fisher <lfisher@welltron.com> |
|---|---|
| From: | Peter Willingsworth <pwillings@fiestatech.com> |
| Subject: | a venture in Brazil |

Dear Lawrence,

It was great to see you again at the annual convention last week. I was happy to hear that consumer demand has picked up at your company. The fact that the recession seems to be coming to an end is a positive boost for all of us.

I wanted to pick up on our discussion of collaborating on a venture in Brazil. Now that the economy there seems to be expanding, no doubt your company is interested in establishing a presence in the South American market. In fact, I'm confident that our companies could negotiate a deal that is satisfactory for both parties. A recent analysis of the Brazilian market for our products showed that there is a large potential customer base to be targeted. I would expect that within a decade we would have an advantage over other companies and be able to show good profits for our stockholders. The difficult part of the venture is determining how the exchange rate will change in the future and how that will affect our business strategy.

Let's plan to meet next week to discuss how to proceed with the venture. Any day but Wednesday is good for me. Tuesday afternoon is best. Friday morning is good, too. What works for you?

Best regards,
Peter Willingsworth

1. Where did they meet recently?
   (A) At Peter's company
   (B) At Lawrence's company
   (C) At the annual convention
   (D) In Brazil

2. Why does Peter think Lawrence's company must be interested in a venture in Brazil?
   (A) The economy is getting worse.
   (B) It can develop potential customers.
   (C) Peter is confident.
   (D) Lawrence must analyze the Brazilian market.

3. What will affect their business strategy?
   (A) The future exchange rate
   (B) The advantage over other companies
   (C) Determining the difficult part of the venture
   (D) The profits for their stockholders

4. What day is NOT convenient for Peter?
   (A) Tuesday
   (B) Wednesday
   (C) Thursday
   (D) Friday

---

**解法のポイント**　　　　**手紙やメール問題で注目すべき箇所**

枠外の導入文や形式から手紙やメール形式の問題であることが分かった場合、本文よりもまず先に目を通さなければならないのが、最初と最後に書かれた「差出人・宛先・日付・件名」などの項目だ。これらが質問に関わっていることも多いので、絶対に読み飛ばさないこと。

# Unit 8　Employment & Personnel

受動態

## Part 1　ターゲット　　　受動態の表現に慣れよう

Part 1では、進行形以外にも、〈受動態〉の表現も頻出だ。〈受動態〉とは、主語が他の人や物によって動作を受ける表現で、「be動詞＋過去分詞」の形で「〜が…される」と訳される。写っている人や物の状況が〈受動態〉で表現されている可能性も頭に入れて、写真から情報を読み取ろう。

Listen and fill in the blanks for each sentence. Then choose the statement that best describes what you see in the picture.　　CheckLink

1.　　　　　　　　　　　　　　　DL 44　CD2-61 ～ CD2-65

(A) The men are (　　　　　　)
　　(　　　　　) a bench.
(B) The men are (　　　　　　)
　　(　　　　) the park.
(C) The men are (　　　　　　)
　　(　　　　).
(D) The men are (　　　　　　)
　　(　　　　　　) each other.

Choose the statement that best describes what you see in the picture.

2.　　　　　　　CheckLink　DL 45　CD2-66

(A)　(B)　(C)　(D)

### 解法のポイント　　　"by 〜" の省略

受動態の基本形は「be動詞＋過去分詞＋by〜」だが、誰によって、あるいは何によってされている［された］のかがはっきりしない場合や、特に明確にする必要がない場合は省略されるので、by〜が聞こえてこなくても、受動態である可能性は大いにある。写真の状況から判断しよう。

# Part 3

日常生活やビジネスの現場で使用される単語・表現を覚えておこう

Part 3では、日常生活や職場での会話が圧倒的に多い。このような場面で使用される単語や表現を覚えておくと、会話の場面や2人の話者の関係を推測したり、会話の内容を把握したりすることがかなり容易になる。

Listen to the conversation and fill in the blanks. Then choose the best answer to each question.

W: I (1.        ) there is a (2.        ) (3.        ) in your company. Is the (4.        ) still open?

M: Yeah. We have a plan to (5.        ) (6.        ) a new (7.        ) (8.        ) next year, so now we're looking for an (9.        ) (10.        ).

W: My college friend is (11.        ) in the job. She is a very nice person to work with. Also, she has a (12.        ) in media and (13.        ) in editing and proofreading.

M: (14.        ) (15.        ). Can you ask her to send her (16.        ) which (17.        ) her contact (18.        )?

1. What are the speakers talking about?
   (A) Job vacancy
   (B) Magazine subscription
   (C) The editor-in-chief
   (D) High degree of competition

2. What is the man's company going to do next year?
   (A) Recruit a media consultant
   (B) Open a local restaurant
   (C) Hire an assistant photographer
   (D) Launch a new magazine

3. What will the woman's friend probably send to the man?
   (A) A magazine which she edited
   (B) Her résumé
   (C) Information about local shops
   (D) Her tax certificate

Unit 8 Employment & Personnel   71

Listen to the conversation and choose the best answer to each question.

**4.** What are the speakers discussing?
   (A) Headquarters relocation
   (B) Investment in research and development
   (C) A performance-based pay system
   (D) Promotion and transfer

**5.** Who will move to the headquarters?
   (A) The man   (B) The woman   (C) David   (D) Martin

**6.** What does the woman say about Martin?
   (A) He is pleased with his performance.
   (B) He is disappointed he couldn't take up the post as director.
   (C) He isn't satisfied with the results of the experiment.
   (D) He is impatient to move to Chicago.

### 解法のポイント　　初級から中級レベルのビジネス英語に慣れる

TOEICでは専門的な業務に関わる内容までは基本的に出題されない一方で、求人・雇用・異動・転勤・リストラ・退職・会議・出張・プレゼンといった、企業や職場で一般的に行われる業務や仕事の場面・状況は頻繁に登場する。部署名や役職名を英語で覚えたり、社内英語の語彙を増やしたりして、ビジネス英語に徐々に慣れよう。

## Part 6　ターゲット　　受動態をマスターしよう

受動態は、基本形を少し発展させるだけですぐ応用問題が解けるようになる文法項目だ。まず、by以外の前置詞を使う動詞を覚え、次に、時制・助動詞・不定詞などが一緒につくと、どういう形になるかを確認しよう。それほど問題のバリエーションもなく、比較的理解しやすいところなので、ぜひ攻略してほしい。

**Questions 1-4** refer to the following e-mail.

To: Powell Boyle <powellb@hardensoft.com>
From: Nick Sandon <sandon@newtech.com>
Date: January 25
Re: Revised Version of New Employee Orientation Schedule

Hello Powell,

I presume that you already received all the paperwork required for the -------

**1.** (A) occupation
(B) qualification
(C) opportunity
(D) procedure

to join our company and the schedule for the new employee orientation, but I am sending you this email to inform you that we rearranged the orientation for February 9.

It was ------- planned for February 1. Parts of our building have ------- for

**2.** (A) conversely
(B) alternatively
(C) originally
(D) instead

**3.** (A) close
(B) closed
(C) been closed
(D) to be closing

maintenance since last month. The work was to be completed before January 30, but the completion ------- due to the lack of materials.

**4.** (A) would have been delayed
(B) delays
(C) will be delayed
(D) was delaying

This being the case, we changed the date of the orientation to February 9 but the start time and the meeting place are the same. Please refer to the attached file for the revised schedule just in case. I look forward to meeting you soon.

Best regards,

Nick Sandon
Human Resources Department

---

**解法のポイント**　　　複数の日付に注目

Part 6の時制に関する設問は、空所を含む英文を読んだだけでは解答を選べない。必ず〈時間〉に言及する表現が前後に出ているので、時の流れを追いながら読み進めよう。メールや手紙タイプの問題では、送信日を起点にして、本文に出てくる日付の時制を考えること。

Unit 8 **Employment & Personnel** ○ 73

# Part 7　ターゲット　　　ビジネス文書に慣れよう①

Part 7ではビジネス文書が頻出だが、ビジネス経験がない大学生にはなかなか馴染みがない。最初は日本語でも良いので、普段から新聞・書籍・雑誌・インターネットなどで、ビジネスの基本的な知識やビジネスに関連する用語や表現をおさえておこう。【→巻末 Key Vocabulary】

**Questions 1-4** refer to the following e-mail.

| To: | Nancy Chang <nchang@greenecom.com> |
|---|---|
| From: | Tony Brookfield <tb3@greenecom.com> |
| Subject: | transfer |

Dear Nancy,

Congratulations! This morning I got an unofficial e-mail from Eric Lambert, the manager of the Personnel Department, saying that your request to transfer to headquarters in New York has been approved. As someone who recommended you, I don't find it surprising. It's well-deserved recognition of your contribution to the company. Your sales performance over the last eight years has been outstanding. The timing was also good, since headquarters was recruiting a salesperson to fill a vacancy. All in all, it worked out better than I had thought.

The manager of the Sales Department of the New York office, Patrick Liu, will contact you in the next few days and send you some important information regarding your new position. If you have any questions, please ask Catherine Cohen in our Personnel Department. She will help you complete all official documents. You start working in New York on September 1. I cannot believe that you will be leaving us in a month! Nancy, the people in the Sales Department of the Sydney office will miss you, but we wish you the best of luck in your new job.

All the best,
Tony

1. What did Nancy request?
   (A) A pay raise
   (B) A promotion
   (C) A transfer
   (D) Flextime

2. Who will contact Nancy?
   (A) Eric Lambert
   (B) Patrick Liu
   (C) Catherine Cohen
   (D) Tony Brookfield

3. When did Tony write this e-mail?
   (A) In April
   (B) In June
   (C) In August
   (D) In October

4. Which is one of the reasons why Nancy's request has been approved?
   (A) There was a job opening.
   (B) The company's revenue increased.
   (C) Patrick Liu helped her complete documents.
   (D) She has worked in Sydney for eight years.

---

**解法のポイント**　　ビジネス文書で注目すべき2点

手紙であれ、メールであれ、①文書の発信者と受信者は誰か、②文書を発信している目的は何かを確認しよう。最初の段落でこれらに関する重要な情報が得られることが多いが、メールの場合、subject「件名」を読むだけで、本文の大まかな内容が想像できる場合もある。

# Unit 9 Office Work & Correspondence

分詞・分詞構文

## Part 1　ターゲット　発音が同じ単語や表現に注意しよう

Part 1では、Part 3やPart 4のように質問や選択肢の英文があるわけではないので、とにかく流れてくる音声だけで答えを出さなければならない。したがって、一度聞いた文の意味を即座に、正確に理解しなければならないが、それを困難にするのが「同じ音で意味が異なる」語句や表現だ。きちんと意味を考えながら、聞き分けよう。

Listen and fill in the blanks for each sentence. Then choose the statement that best describes what you see in the picture.

**1.**　　　　　　　　　　　　　　　　　　CheckLink　DL 50　CD2-79 ~ CD2-83

(A) The woman's (　　　　　) the (　　　　) to use the phone.
(B) The woman's phone is (　　　　) the (　　　　).
(C) The woman's (　　　　　　) an (　　　　　) file through her phone.
(D) The woman's (　　　　　) the phone on the (　　　　).

Choose the statement that best describes what you see in the picture.

**2.**　　　　　　　　　　　　　　CheckLink　DL 51　CD2-84

(A)　(B)　(C)　(D)

### 解法のポイント　　省略されて読まれる語に注意

「同じ音で意味が異なる」といえば、ate / eight や hear / here などの同音異義語を思い浮かべるが、短縮形が同じ音というのもある。例えば、the man's と読まれても、the man's（所有格）、また the man is や the man has の短縮形の可能性があるし、you'd と読まれても、you would や you had の短縮形の可能性がある。直後にくる語の品詞や文脈まで気を配ろう。

76

# Part 4 ターゲット　　留守番電話に慣れよう

Part 4で頻出の留守番電話形式の問題では、「誰から誰に、何の目的での連絡か」を把握することが大事になる。最初に話し手が自分は何者かを名乗るので聞き落さないようにして、話し手と聞き手の関係を把握しよう。また、話し手、あるいは聞き手がこの後何をするか（しなければならないか）を問う問題も頻出なので、終盤の内容にも注意したい。

**Listen to the short talk and fill in the blanks. Then choose the best answer to each question.**   CheckLink   DL 52   CD2-85 ~ CD2-88

Hi Jason, this is Katie from the (1. _____) (2. _____). Our next (3. _____) on the new accounting (4. _____) was supposed to be this (5. _____) (6. _____), but David has to (7. _____) a meeting in our (8. _____) office on that day. He is the (9. _____) (10. _____) in the next workshop, so I (11. _____) to (12. _____) it to (13. _____), next week, (14. _____) 21. And there's another change: we (15. _____) (16. _____) (17. _____) the meeting room on the second floor because our usual room on the (18. _____) (19. _____) will be used for another (20. _____) on Monday. Could you (21. _____) this information to the other members? I have to (22. _____) my office now, so please call my (23. _____) Martin Smith if you have any questions. Thanks, Jason!

**1.** Why was the workshop postponed?   DL 53   CD2-89
 (A) David is away for business.
 (B) The launch date of the new accounting software is delayed.
 (C) Jason has to attend another meeting in London.
 (D) Their usual meeting room is booked by another committee.

**2.** Who is the main presenter in the next workshop?
 (A) Martin　(B) Katie　(C) David　(D) Jason

**3.** What will the speaker do after leaving this message?
 (A) Pass this information to the other members
 (B) Have a meeting with Martin
 (C) Be out of her office
 (D) Go back to working in her office

Unit 9 Office Work & Correspondence ○ 77

Listen to the short talk and choose the best answer to each question.

**4.** What is the purpose of the message?
(A) To notify they are sending a bill
(B) To ask for contact information
(C) To explain their new opening hours
(D) To make a contract with Mr. Gordon

**5.** What is Mr. Gordon asked to do?
(A) Change his address  (C) Visit Hudson Books
(B) Pay shipping costs  (D) Call Hudson Books

**6.** When is the store open?
(A) 10 a.m. on weekdays
(B) 11 a.m. on weekends
(C) 5 p.m. on weekdays
(D) 6 p.m. on weekends

---

**解法のポイント**　　　音声の順番で質問に取り組む

Part 4は一人が長く話すタイプの音声問題なので、すべてを聞き取るのは難しく、TOEICに慣れていない人は途中で聞き取りをあきらめてしまう。しかし基本的に、質問は読まれる音声の順に出題されるので、音声を聞く前に質問を読んでおくようにすれば正答率を上げることができる。

## Part 5　ターゲット　分詞と分詞構文をマスターしよう

Choose the best answer to complete the sentence.

**1.** 限定用法：The clerk ------- at the copier is going to leave this company because she is tired of her dull routine work.
(A) standard   (B) stands   (C) standing   (D) stood

**2.** 限定用法：The solution to the leak of confidential information ------- by the committee was just a stopgap measure.
(A) adopting   (B) adopted   (C) adopter   (D) adapter

3. 人の感情・様態：Her supervisor was ------- by her failure in this important presentation and felt himself blush.
   (A) embarrassed      (C) to embarrass
   (B) embarrassing     (D) embarrassment

4. 物事の性質：Her failure in this important presentation was ------- to her supervisor and made him blush.
   (A) embarrassed      (C) to embarrass
   (B) embarrassing     (D) embarrassment

5. 分詞構文：------- how to deal with complaints well, Sophia asked her senior colleague for advice.
   (A) Knowing not      (C) No knowing
   (B) Not knowing      (D) Not to know

6. 分詞構文：------- what the postage was on the parcel, the post office clerk measured it with a ruler and weighed it.
   (A) Ask   (B) To ask   (C) Asked   (D) Asking

7. 分詞構文：------- the interim report my subordinate submitted, half of our sales representatives are unlikely to meet their sales quotas this month.
   (A) Judging from         (C) Granting that
   (B) Generally speaking   (D) Weather permitting

8. 使役：She confirmed the number of participants for her seminar, prepared the handouts, and then got them ------- by her assistant.
   (A) staple   (B) staples   (C) stapled   (D) stapler

9. 付帯状況：When his secretary was about to talk to the vice president, he was thinking about something with his eyes ------- and his chin resting in his hand.
   (A) close   (B) closing   (C) closed   (D) closely

10. 付帯状況：The invoice says that the total price of the office supplies and stationery we ordered is $400 with the postage and packing -------.
    (A) to include   (B) includes   (C) including   (D) included

---

**解法のポイント　　分詞構文の問題は、主語を意識する**

分詞構文の問題で空所の前に名詞がない場合、分詞構文の意味上の主語と主節の主語は一致する。"------- from a distance, the hotel looks like a castle." という問題では、空所前に名詞がないので、主語は主節の the hotel と同じということだ。ホテルには「目」が付いておらず、「見る側」か「見られる側」では、「見られる側」になるので、空所には Seen が入る。

Unit 9　Office Work & Correspondence　79

# Part 7　ターゲット　　ビジネス文書に慣れよう②

Part 7に出題されるビジネス文書には、手紙・メール・回覧文などのパターンがあり、その内容は業務連絡、会議やイベントの日時や場所の告知、異動、会社の移転や改築の通知など多岐にわたる。練習問題をこなしてこれらのパターンに慣れよう。

**Questions 1-4** refer to the following memo.

**TO**: All contracted part-time employees
**FROM**: Wendy Taylor, HR Manager
**SUBJECT**: Perfect Attendance Bonus Program

We would like to inform you that we have adopted a new Perfect Attendance Bonus Program. Contracted part-time employees who have perfect attendance will receive a $250 bonus.

—**Qualification**
An employee must have perfect attendance during the contract year to qualify for the bonus. This means that the employee did not take any sick leave, was always on time and did not leave early.

—**How to receive the bonus**
You should complete a Perfect Attendance Bonus Request Form. The request is due within 30 days from you completing a one-year period of perfect attendance. If you do not submit a form within 30 days, your request will be denied.

—**Where to get the Perfect Attendance Bonus Request Form**
You can pick up a Perfect Attendance Bonus Request Form from your immediate supervisor. You can also download the form from the internal website.

—**Who should I submit the Perfect Attendance Bonus Request Form to**
You should submit the form to your immediate supervisor. The supervisor will review and sign off on the form and submit it to the Human Resources Manager.

Please contact me if you have any questions. I can be reached at extension 2102.

Wendy Taylor
HR Manager

1. What is the main purpose of the memorandum?
   (A) To explain how to take sick leave
   (B) To warn contracted employees not to be absent
   (C) To encourage employees to attend a meeting
   (D) To give information about the perfect attendance bonus

2. Who can get the special $250 bonus?
   (A) Human resources managers that have improved existing programs
   (B) All employees who completed a sick leave request form
   (C) Contracted part-time employees with perfect attendance for a year
   (D) Immediate supervisors at the Human Resources Department

3. What should employees do if they don't completely understand the program?
   (A) Read working regulations
   (B) Call Wendy Taylor
   (C) Discuss it with their supervisors
   (D) Check the internal website

4. What is true about the application process?
   (A) The Perfect Attendance can be approved even if employees are tardy or leave early.
   (B) A Perfect Attendance Bonus Request Form cannot be downloaded.
   (C) Employees can request Perfect Attendance Bonus anytime when qualified.
   (D) Employees should hand in the completed request form to their supervisor first.

---

**解法のポイント**　　ひとつの単語にとらわれすぎない

英語の文書を読んでいると、必ず見慣れない単語や難解な表現が出てくる。しかし、いくつか分からない単語や表現があるからといって、文書の内容が全く理解できないということはない。落ち着いて前後の文脈をきちんとたどれば、文書の全体的な内容を把握することができる。

# Unit 10 Health & the Environment

不定詞・動名詞

## Part 1　ターゲット　発音が似ている単語に注意しよう

(A)〜(D)の選択肢に、似たような音の単語が複数使われている問題がある。何となく聞いているだけだと、簡単にだまされてしまうので、英語独特の発音を意識しながら、リスニングの練習に取り組もう。

Listen and fill in the blanks for each sentence. Then choose the statement that best describes what you see in the picture.

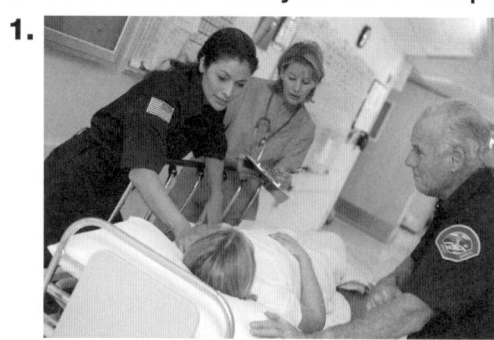

DL 56　CD3-01 〜 CD3-05

1.

(A) The paramedics are (　　　　　) (　　　　) the corridor.
(B) The paramedics are (　　　　　) to examine the (　　　　).
(C) The paramedics are waiting for an (　　　　　) (　　　　　).
(D) The paramedics are taking an (　　　　) of their arms.

Choose the statement that best describes what you see in the picture.

2.　　　　　　　　　　　　　　CheckLink　DL 57　CD3-06

(A)　(B)　(C)　(D)

### 解法のポイント　　自分で発音してみる

walk / work, travel / trouble, personal / personnel などの発音が似ている語は、リスニングの練習をしているだけではなかなか聞き取れるようにはならないが、自分で正しく発音できるようになると聞き分けられるようになる。音声を真似して音読あるのみだ。

82

# Part 2 ターゲット　変則的な応答問題に注意しよう

Part 2のひとつ目の問いかけは、必ずしも疑問文とは限らない。平叙文に対する受け答えをしなければならないこともあれば、疑問文に対して疑問文で答えることもある。また、orを使って二者択一をさせる疑問文や、付加疑問文なども出題される。実際のやり取りとして最も自然な応答を選ぼう。

Listen and fill in the blanks for each sentence. Then choose the best response to each question or statement. CheckLink　DL 58〜60　CD3-07

CD3-08 〜 CD3-11

1. Do not forget to (　　　) the (　　　) out of the socket when you are not using the (　　　).
   (A) Where (　　　)(　　　)(　　　) this cable into?
   (B) You are (　　　), (　　　)(　　　)?
   (C) I can't (　　　)(　　　) buy the appliance.

CD3-12 〜 CD3-15

2. I'm having (　　　)(　　　) downloading the application for paid leave.
   (A) Just click this (　　　) to download the (　　　).
   (B) I (　　　) for (　　　).
   (C) It's (　　　)(　　　) live there again.

CD3-16 〜 CD3-19

3. Why don't you go _____?
   (A) This medicine does not _____.
   (B) The dentist _____.
   (C) I hate _____.

Listen to the question or statement and the three responses. Then choose the best response. CheckLink　DL 61　CD3-20

4. (A)　(B)　(C)

解法のポイント　文の奥にあるメッセージを読み取る

平叙文に対する応答は正解が分かりにくい。例えば「この部屋、暑いですね」という平叙文は単なる事実報告に聞こえるが、Part 2は相手の応答を問う問題なので、実際には「エアコンを入れましょうか」「窓を開けましょうか」といった反応を期待しているわけだ。平叙文での問いかけ問題は、文字通りの内容を受け取るのではなく、奥に隠れたメッセージを読み取ってほしい。

# Part 5 ターゲット　不定詞と動名詞をマスターしよう

Choose the best answer to complete the sentence.

**1.** 形容詞的用法：The factory is going to introduce exhaust gas cleaning equipment ------- toxic fine particles and reduce air pollution.
(A) remove　(B) removal　(C) remover　(D) to remove

**2.** 仮主語と動詞の目的語：It is necessary for us ------- a vehicle which emits a large quantity of carbon dioxide if we are seriously considering stopping global warming.
(A) to avoid for choosing　　(C) avoiding to choose
(B) to avoid choosing　　(D) avoiding to be chosen

**3.** 不定詞と動名詞：The physician advised him to give up ------- immediately in order to improve the condition of his heart.
(A) to drink and smoke　　(C) drinking and to smoke
(B) to drink and smoking　　(D) drinking and smoking

**4.** 不定詞と動名詞：Remember ------- this medicine three times a day after meals according to the prescription.
(A) take　(B) taken　(C) to take　(D) taking

**5.** 疑問詞に続く時：The management is wondering ------- a cafeteria benefits plan instead of conventional welfare like social insurance, or a family or housing allowance.
(A) about whether introduction　(C) whether to introduce
(B) of whether introducing　(D) whether we should be introduced

**6.** 原形不定詞：The nutritionist helps obese patients ------- weight by calculating daily calorie intake and offering advice on a balanced diet.
(A) lose　(B) lost　(C) to losing　(D) loss

**7.** 使役：I was in bed with such a high fever that I had my sister ------- up my son at the day care.
(A) to pick　(B) picks　(C) pick　(D) picked

8. 結果程度：Since some treatments and surgical operations are not covered by health insurance, they are ------- for ordinary people to pay at their own expense.
   (A) enough cheap　　(C) too cheap
   (B) expensive enough　　(D) too expensive

9. 目的：Mr. Vincent wore a mask whenever he was on a commuter train or in a crowd ------- to catch the flu.
   (A) so as not　(B) such as　(C) in case　(D) not in order

10. 慣用表現：When it comes to ------- your remaining paid vacation as sick leave, you must submit a medical certificate from your doctor to your immediate supervisor.
    (A) use　(B) to use　(C) using　(D) usage

### 解法のポイント
**目的語が不定詞か動名詞かで意味が異なる他動詞に注意**

他動詞は、目的語が〈不定詞〉か〈動名詞〉かで意味が変わってくる場合がある。
不定詞は「まだ起こっていない事柄 or まだ行っていない行為」
動名詞は「すでに起こった事柄 or すでに行った行為」
を表すという違いがある。

　a. I forgot to buy copy paper.
　b. I forgot buying copy paper.

a. は「私はコピー用紙を買うのを忘れた」という意味でコピー用紙は未購入、b. は「私はコピー用紙を買ったことを忘れていた」という意味でコピー用紙は購入済み、ということになる。

## Part 7　ターゲット　速読力をつけよう

それなりに単語の勉強もして、アドバイス通りの順番で解いているのに Part 7でスコアが取れないという人に足りないのは、ずばりスピードだ。「返り読み」せず、一文一文を読み進める練習を重ねて、全体のスピードアップをはかろう。

**Questions 1-4** refer to the following notice.

### 25ᵗʰ Tree-planting Campaign by NPO Trees for the Future Calling for Volunteers

With the growing population, the number of cars in our city has been skyrocketing, causing many serious environmental problems with their toxic emissions. These are unwelcome guests in our community. Let's do something about it and protect our city.

From the beginning of next month, we, NPO Trees for the Future, will conduct our annual tree-planting campaign. So far, we have planted more than 2,000 trees in the city. To fight for a healthy environment, however, we need more trees. Therefore, we welcome volunteers to help with our campaign.

This is our 25ᵗʰ anniversary, so we are inviting an internationally famous expert—Andrew Scott. He is the president of an environmental NPO encouraging eco-friendly city planning and advanced waste recycling systems.

*For further information visit*
*http://npotreesforthefuture.org*

1. What is the purpose of the notice?
   (A) To let people know how dangerous cars are
   (B) To urge people to volunteer
   (C) To protect tropical rainforests
   (D) To invite Andrew Scott

2. Who most likely is Andrew Scott?
   (A) A representative of an NPO
   (B) A mayor
   (C) A presidential candidate
   (D) A web designer

3. What is stated about the campaign?
   (A) It accepts no volunteers.
   (B) It is assisted by a conductor.
   (C) It causes serious environmental problems.
   (D) It is held once a year.

4. What should you probably do if you want to work as a volunteer for this organization?
   (A) Fill out an application form
   (B) Make a phone call
   (C) Use the Internet
   (D) Send a fax

---

◀解法のポイント　　　　　時間配分を刻み込む　　　　　→ → →

Part 7全問を解くのにどのくらいのスピードが必要かというと、「質問1問につき1分」。つまり質問が3問ある文章は3分以内に読み終わらなければならないということだ。そこで普段の勉強でぜひ活用してほしいのがタイマーだ。タイマーで細かく時間を区切って練習すると、本番の緊張感を伴いつつ、時間配分を身体に刻むことができるので、速読練習に大変効果的だ。

# Unit 11 Finance & Banking

代名詞・関係詞

## Part 1　ターゲット　多義語に注意しよう

Part 1を解答するうえで克服しなければならないのが、多義語を含む問題である。同じ単語でもさまざまな意味を持つ単語には十分警戒して、誤答を選ばないようにしよう。

Listen and fill in the blanks for each sentence. Then choose the statement that best describes what you see in the picture.

CheckLink　DL 62　CD3-21 ～ CD3-25

1.
(A) The man on the left is (　　　　) a (　　　　).
(B) The man on the right is (　　　　) (　　　　).
(C) Glass windows are (　　　　) (　　　　).
(D) A laptop computer is placed (　　　) (　　　) (　　　) of a door.

Choose the statement that best describes what you see in the picture.

CheckLink　DL 63　CD3-26

2.
(A)　(B)　(C)　(D)

### 解法のポイント　　前後の単語がヒント

よく登場する多義語にはbank「銀行／土手」やchange「おつり／変える」などがある。その単語だけに反応しないで、ひとつの文全体をよく聞き取り、その文が表している状況を理解すること。

# Part 3 ターゲット  長文のリスニングに慣れよう

Part 4だけでなく、Part 3の会話問題でも、以前と比較するとやや長めの長文のリスニングが出題されるようになってきた。会話が長くなれば、それだけ流れてくる情報も多くなる。会話が流れる前に質問と選択肢に目を通しておきたいが、音声が流れてきたら読むのをやめて、聞くことにひたすら集中したい。

**Listen to the conversation and fill in the blanks. Then choose the best answer to each question.** CheckLink  DL 64  CD3-27 ~ CD3-31

W: Did you see the (1.        ) (2.        )?
M: Yeah. And I also read our (3.        ) (4.        ) (5.        )
   (6.        ) at yesterday's meeting. And I carefully checked the
   (7.        ) (8.        ) for this month and the (9.        )
   for the next (10.        ).
W: What did you think about them? I think the (11.        ) is very
   (12.        ) about his prospect.
M: You're probably right. If we cannot sell our (13.        ) (14.        )
   to large (15.        ), it will be impossible to (16.        ) our sales
   (17.        ).

1. What are the speakers mainly talking about?  DL 65  CD3-32
   (A) The annual meeting
   (B) The sales report
   (C) The quarterly journal
   (D) The sales staff

2. How does the woman feel about the manager?
   (A) He is positive about his outlook.
   (B) He is pessimistic about the sales figures.
   (C) He is angry about the performance.
   (D) He is disappointed with the company.

3. What is the man worried about?
   (A) They have to postpone the release of their new product.
   (B) The company he has been working for will go bankrupt.
   (C) The sales target cannot be reached.
   (D) The manager will quit this month.

Unit 11 Finance & Banking

Listen to the conversation and choose the best answer to each question.

**4.** Where is the conversation taking place?
(A) In an airport
(C) In a bank
(B) In an accountant's office
(D) In a driving school

**5.** Which of the following is mentioned as identification?
(A) Insurance card
(C) Credit bill
(B) Student ID card
(D) Driver's license

**6.** According to the woman, how much does the man have to deposit?
(A) $10   (B) $50   (C) $100   (D) $1,000

### 解法のポイント　全部聞き取れなくても焦らない

Part 3ではひとつの会話につき、3つの質問がある。しかし、流れてくる音声をすべて聞き取り、内容を完全に把握することはかなり難しいので、最初は3問中1〜2問を確実に正解することを目指そう。聞き落としがあっても慌てず、質問されていることを聞き取って、落ち着いて答えられるようにしたい。

## Part 5　ターゲット　代名詞の用法を確認して、関係代名詞と関係副詞をマスターしよう

Choose the best answer to complete the sentence.

**1.** 代名詞の格：I went to the ATM to withdraw some money from my savings account, but I couldn't remember ------- PIN number.
(A) I   (B) my   (C) me   (D) mine

**2.** 代名詞の格：As the financial condition of our company is sound, our main bank will finance ------- with fifty thousand dollars at a lower interest rate.
(A) we   (B) our   (C) us   (D) ourselves

**3.** 再帰代名詞：Although the accountant has grown and is now very reliable, the accounting manager never fails to check the accounting books -------.
(A) him   (B) his   (C) himself   (D) on his

**4.** 人々：------- in charge of housing loans are on a business trip. Please call again during business hours at the beginning of next week.
(A) Our clerk   (B) Those   (C) Someone   (D) A person

**5.** 主格：Ms. Beckman is a consultant ------- hired to give us a detailed analysis of our management style and provide appropriate advice.
(A) which have   (B) who has   (C) that are   (D) who was

**6.** 目的格：We handed in the balance sheet for the previous fiscal year ------- she had prepared and analyzed carefully.
(A) what   (B) whom   (C) which   (D) of that

**7.** 非制限用法：That virtual currency exchange went bankrupt with a 65 billion yen debt, ------- some people had predicted in advance.
(A) which   (B) what   (C) that   (D) thing

**8.** 〜こと：------- you need to do right now is to repay your debt. The reminder says you'll get charged late fees if you don't transfer the payment by the due date.
(A) Which   (B) What   (C) That   (D) Thing

**9.** 場所・時：2012 was the turning point ------- eGulf Inc. finally went into the black and posted a net profit of three billion dollars.
(A) when   (B) which   (C) why   (D) who

**10.** そのようにして：Silver Hawks Electronics had been in the red for five consecutive quarters but tried to reduce its expenditures drastically. That's ------- it escaped the situation where liabilities exceed assets.
(A) a method that   (B) by the way   (C) the means of   (D) how

---

**解法のポイント**　　まず先行詞を確認すること

関係詞の問題を解く時は、まず先行詞が何かを考えよう。先行詞が見当たらない→ what、先行詞が場所→（ほぼ）where など、すぐに答えが出る場合がある。

## Part 7 ターゲット　通知文書に慣れよう

Part 7では、情報の共有・宣伝・変更・警告などの通知文も頻出問題だ。通知対象の明記→通知内容→付随する注意点→特記事項の順に書いてあるので、今まで通り先に質問に目を通して、どこに狙いを定めて読むか目星を付けてから、流れに沿って効率的に読もう。

**Questions 1-4** refer to the following website.　　CheckLink

---

**FIRST TRUST BANK**

| home | about us | customer service | locations | investor relations |

### FRAUD PROTECTION

We want to inform our valued customers about recent hoax emails. These emails use our bank logo and copyright to propose various financial investments, such as short-term and long-term savings. By clicking on the link provided in the email the customer is taken to a website that explains the details of the offer. The website, however, is not an official bank website. Customers are asked to enter their information, including their account number and PIN so as to check the balance. This is an attempt to illegally obtain your personal information and withdraw funds from your account.

*It is important to note that until now there have not been any confirmed reports of customers falling victim to this hoax. We do, however, ask customers to be cautious. And as a reminder, our bank does not propose investments by email, nor do we require you to send any personal information to us over the Internet.

▶ Learn more about hoax emails and phishing scams
▶ Examples of scams

1. Why was the notice written?
   (A) To announce the bank's new logo
   (B) To propose short-term savings
   (C) To warn about a hoax e-mail
   (D) To open the bank's website

2. What kind of information are customers asked to enter on the website?
   (A) Account number
   (B) Fund balance
   (C) Copyright
   (D) E-mail address

3. How does the customer get to the unofficial bank website?
   (A) By sending an e-mail to the bank
   (B) By withdrawing their funds
   (C) By logging in to the bank's official website
   (D) By clicking on the link in the e-mail

4. How many customers have reported financial losses due to this hoax?
   (A) None
   (B) One
   (C) Some
   (D) Many

---

**解法のポイント**　　　　言い換えを見逃さない　　　→→→

リスニングセクションにも共通することだが、Part 7の本文で使われている言葉が、質問や選択肢で言い換えられていることがよくある。リスニングセクションではうっかり聞き逃すこともありがちだが、Part 7では文字で読めるので、見逃さないようにしたい。

# Unit 12 Law & Administration

比較構文

## Part 1 ターゲット　　専門用語に慣れよう

「法律」や「行政」といった分野は普段の生活の中でなかなか目にする機会がないかもしれないが、高得点を狙うならぜひとも押さえておきたい。特に法律の分野では独特な単語や表現も登場するので、英字新聞やニュースサイトで「事件記事」などに目を通す習慣をつけよう。

Listen and fill in the blanks for each sentence. Then choose the statement that best describes what you see in the picture.　CheckLink

1.　DL 68　CD3-39 ~ CD3-43

(A) The road is (　　　) (　　　) trees on both sides.
(B) The road is (　　　) (　　　) tourists.
(C) The speed limit (　　　) is (　　　) (　　　) the (　　　).
(D) A police officer is (　　　) (　　　) at the intersection.

Choose the statement that best describes what you see in the picture.

2.　CheckLink　DL 69　CD3-44

(A)　(B)　(C)　(D)

### 解法のポイント　　専門的な語句を聞く機会を増やそう

法律や行政などの専門的な分野の語句や表現は「読んで分かる」だけでは不十分だ。リスニングセクションで出題されてもいいように、専門的な語句や表現を「聞いて分かる」レベルまで引き上げたい。音声付きの web 辞書や電子辞書で単語を調べたら「音声ボタン」を押して発音を確認すること。音を聞くだけでその語の意味が頭に浮かぶようになるまで、繰り返し聞いて、自分でも発音しよう。

# Part 4　報道・ニュースに慣れよう

Part 4の10個の音声中、1～3個は報道・ニュースの音声が出題されている。その中で天気予報は比較的簡単で、交通情報も攻略しやすいが、ニュースは少しレベルが高い。質問の先読みやショートトークの音声が流れる前の導入部をうまく活用して、なんとかついて行こう。

Listen to the short talk and fill in the blanks. Then choose the best answer to each question.

Hello, ETS radio listeners. This is Rebecca Pierson with (1.　　　) (2.　　　). Josh Martin, a (3.　　　) with the Dawson Symphony Orchestra, is on (4.　　　) this week on a charge of disturbing the peace after his (5.　　　) (6.　　　) him of harassing her by practicing the violin for (7.　　　) (8.　　　) (9.　　　) hours a day. The (10.　　　) lived below Martin in an (11.　　　) from 2010 to (12.　　　) and (13.　　　) that she eventually had to (14.　　　) out because she could not (15.　　　) to hear the sound of the violin (16.　　　) (17.　　　). (18.　　　) (19.　　　) the plaintiff's (20.　　　), it sometimes (21.　　　) the 50-decibel limit set for musical (22.　　　) at night in the (23.　　　) area of Dawson City. The (24.　　　) claims that he did not play at night because he gave violin lessons in other towns.

**1.** Who is the defendant?

(A) A pianist　　(C) A real-estate office
(B) A violinist　　(D) A composer

**2.** What is the claim of the plaintiff?

(A) Martin did not stop playing the violin in spite of her complaint.
(B) Martin has not paid his rent for 2 years.
(C) She had to move because of her neighbor's noise.
(D) She suffered hearing loss from 2010 to 2012.

**3.** According to Josh Martin, what was he doing at night?

(A) Giving lessons in other towns
(B) Playing the violin for less than an hour
(C) Receiving lessons out of the town
(D) Tuning his violin

Unit 12　Law & Administration　95

Listen to the short talk and choose the best answer to each question.

CheckLink    DL 72, 73    CD3-50 ~ CD3-53    CD3-54

**4.** How many times was Mr. Hamilton re-elected?
   (A) Once    (B) Twice    (C) Three times    (D) Never

**5.** What was Mr. Anderson's previous occupation?
   (A) Professor    (B) Mayor    (C) Councilman    (D) Lawyer

**6.** Why is Mr. Anderson popular?
   (A) He is younger than Mr. Hamilton.
   (B) He supports women's participation in society.
   (C) He is concerned about citizens' opinions.
   (D) He is supported by the younger generation.

---

**解法のポイント**　　　　Part 4も導入部を逃さない

Questions ○○ through △△ refer to the following □□. の□の導入部に announcement が入れば「空港や駅でのアナウンス」や「社内放送」、telephone message なら「留守番電話」、advertisement なら「広告」、talk なら「博物館や施設のツアーガイド」や「スピーチ」、news report や broadcast なら「ニュース」となる。ジャンルが分かっているだけでも心の準備がしやすくなるので、集中して導入部を聞き取ってほしい。

---

# Part 6　ターゲット　　比較構文をマスターしよう

原級・比較級・最上級の基本構文を確認することは言うまでもないが、比較級強調の much, far, even, still「はるかに・さらに」や、最上級強調の much, by far「ずば抜けて・抜群に」などの修飾語までセットで覚えよう。

---

**Questions 1-4** refer to the following article.　　　CheckLink

March 5—The mayor of Morristown has announced the ------- of brand-new

**1.** (A) construction
　　(B) investigation
　　(C) observation
　　(D) compensation

facilities on the former site of Hester Hospital, which was relocated to Greeneville three years ago. The 28 million dollar project will commence from next August and it is expected to take about six months to complete. The new facilities will include a playground for children, a dog run, and a park. Colin Williams, who was ------- mayor for the first time last year, has started the

     **2.** (A) to elect
       (B) elect
       (C) election
       (D) elected

project, combining community development with greenification, as promised in his campaign.

This announced project will likely be opposed by a citizen group who ------- to

         **3.** (A) objected
           (B) spoke
           (C) went
           (D) opposed

the previous plan to relocate Hester Hospital to a larger site, which would have allowed it to double the number of hospital beds.

In fact, relocating the hospital with such high-level facilities has enabled Greeneville to provide better conditions which allow more pregnant women ------- access to a full range of hospital services. On the other hand, there is, at

**4.** (A) fastly
 (B) faster
 (C) fasten
 (D) fastness

present, no hospital in Morristown which has modern facilities for obstetrics and gynecology, like Hester Hospital. The mayor should consider again the negative impact that its relocation has had on Morristown.

---

### 解法のポイント　　和訳の前に構造を確認する

Part 5と同様に、Part 6でも、いきなり日本語から正解を導こうとすることは得策ではない。①空所の位置から文中での働きを確認→②意味を考える、という機械的な解き方で処理すれば、選択肢を絞り込んでから和訳することになるので、解答時間が短縮できるだけでなく、正答率もアップする。

Unit 12　Law & Administration　97

# Part 7　ターゲット　　色々な種類の英文を読もう

TOEICで出題される英文は、形式だけでなく分野もさまざま。自分が慣れていない分野の場合、その英語の専門用語や表現が分からない上に、日本語での基礎知識もないため、全く内容が推測できないということもある。日頃からさまざまな分野の英文に接しておこう。

**Questions 1-4** refer to the following letter.

Mary Arnold
2421 Marks Road
Hartford, CT
06114

September 12, 2015

Dear Ms. Arnold:

　I am writing to inform you of the court date in the matter of Arnold vs. Meade at the Madison County Courthouse. Your complaint against Henry Meade was filed today, and the trial will take place on October 20. We need to talk in our office no later than one week before the day of the trial because we need to go over some final details before the trial commences. I hope you are available on one of the dates and times listed below. Please telephone us as soon as possible to let us know when you are coming.

・ 11:00 a.m. - 12:30 p.m. on September 30
・ 1:30 p.m. - 3:00 p.m. on October 7
・ 10:00 a.m. - 11:30 a.m. on October 10

　My partner Jefferson Jones and I have obtained several reliable witnesses whom we intend to call to the stand. We'll discuss them at our next meeting. You can reach me at 978-5454 whenever you have questions.

Sincerely,

Tony Peterson
Peterson & Jones

1. Who is Tony Peterson?
   (A) A defendant
   (B) A judge
   (C) A witness
   (D) A lawyer

2. When was the suit of Arnold vs. Meade filed?
   (A) September 12
   (B) September 30
   (C) October 7
   (D) October 20

3. The word "commences" in paragraph 1, line 5, is closest in meaning to
   (A) drains
   (B) begins
   (C) rehearses
   (D) breaks

4. What is implied in the letter?
   (A) Ms. Arnold is suing Mr. Meade.
   (B) Mr. Meade complained about Ms. Arnold.
   (C) Ms. Arnold wrote to Mr. Peterson.
   (D) Mr. Meade will see Mr. Jones one week prior to the trial.

---

### 解法のポイント　　見慣れない文書でもトライする価値あり

自分が不慣れな分野の話でも、すぐにあきらめてはいけない。日付や時間・単語の意味を問う問題などは解けるはずなので、とにかく先に質問に目を通すようにしよう。それでもどうしても解けない場合は、「解ける質問以外は飛ばして、思い切って次の文章に移る」というのもアリだ。もちろん、飛ばした質問にもとりあえずマークはしておくこと！

# Review Test 2

## Part 1

CheckLink  CD3-55

Look at the picture and choose the statement that best describes what you see in the picture.

1.

(A)  (B)  (C)  (D)

2.

(A)  (B)  (C)  (D)

100

**3.**

(A)　(B)　(C)　(D)

**4.**

(A)　(B)　(C)　(D)

## Part 2

CheckLink　CD3-56

Listen to the question or statement and the three responses. Then choose the best response to each question or statement.

5. Mark your answer on your answer sheet.　(A)　(B)　(C)
6. Mark your answer on your answer sheet.　(A)　(B)　(C)
7. Mark your answer on your answer sheet.　(A)　(B)　(C)
8. Mark your answer on your answer sheet.　(A)　(B)　(C)
9. Mark your answer on your answer sheet.　(A)　(B)　(C)
10. Mark your answer on your answer sheet.　(A)　(B)　(C)

# Part 3

CheckLink　CD3-57

Listen to the conversations and choose the best answer to each question.

**11.** What are the man and woman discussing?
   (A) Whether the woman will join the seminar
   (B) Who will make a presentation
   (C) Where the seminar will be held
   (D) When the woman will go to the management office

**12.** How does the woman's reply make the man feel?
   (A) Excited   (B) Angry   (C) Disappointed   (D) Delighted

**13.** What will the woman probably do when she returns?
   (A) Go to Tokyo on business
   (B) Organize a special seminar
   (C) Ask Mr. Barnes to hire more employees
   (D) Catch up with the man on the presentation

---

CheckLink　CD3-58

**14.** Where is the conversation probably taking place?
   (A) In the head office            (C) In a pharmacy
   (B) In a pharmaceutical company   (D) In an emergency room

**15.** How does the man feel?
   (A) Sick   (B) Refreshed   (C) Excited   (D) Frightened

**16.** What does the woman ask the man to do?
   (A) Use health insurance
   (B) Take the medicine right now
   (C) Write a prescription for the medicine
   (D) Read the explanation about the drug

# Part 4

Listen to the short talks and choose the best answer to each question.

**17.** What will Dr. Johnson do tomorrow morning?
　(A) Promote sports for the disabled
　(B) Perform an operation
　(C) Attend a conference of the Sports-Medicine Society
　(D) See Dr. Davis' surgery

**18.** When should they tell the conference's organizers if they want to see the operation?
　(A) Before the morning sessions　　(C) After all the sessions
　(B) In the middle of the session　　(D) Tomorrow morning

**19.** What will they do next?
　(A) Undergo Dr. Davis' surgery　　(C) Listen to Dr. Johnson's talk
　(B) Take a break　　(D) Close the conference

---

**20.** What is the main purpose of this speech?
　(A) To announce the company's merger with a Japanese company
　(B) To propose cutbacks in personnel
　(C) To explain the company's history
　(D) To introduce a new CEO

**21.** What job experience has Andrew White had?
　(A) A teacher　　(C) A laboratory director
　(B) An accountant　　(D) A sales representative

**22.** Why did the speaker resign the position?
　(A) He wanted to promote a generation change in management.
　(B) He had to receive medical treatment.
　(C) The company was acquired by a Japanese company.
　(D) He reached the retirement age of seventy.

# Part 5

Choose the best answer to complete the sentence.

**23.** His innocence ------- and he'll be set free if his lawyer can point out major differences between what each witness told the police.
(A) can proved
(B) will improves
(C) may be proven
(D) must be improved

**24.** The bank clerk suggested that we ------- for a short-term loan because the process is quicker and easier.
(A) apply   (B) applied   (C) applicant   (D) application

**25.** The deficits that England and the U.S. suffered in both trade and finance are known ------- the twin deficits.
(A) by   (B) as   (C) for   (D) to

**26.** The ------- suspect was intensively interrogated by the police and finally confessed that he committed the murder.
(A) arrest   (B) arresting   (C) arrested   (D) to arrest

**27.** I finished writing an e-mail and sent it to my boss at home, but I forgot ------- the monthly sales report.
(A) attach   (B) attaching   (C) to attach   (D) attachment

**28.** The CEO of the electronics manufacturer is considering ------- its R&D division to reduce its budget.
(A) downsize   (B) downsized   (C) to downsize   (D) downsizing

**29.** I'm looking forward ------- you at the next workshop on marketing strategies.
(A) see   (B) to see   (C) for seeing   (D) to seeing

**30.** ------- symptoms were similar to those of a common cold, but suddenly I became seriously ill and was taken to the hospital in an ambulance.
(A) I   (B) My   (C) Me   (D) Mine

**31.** More than 10,000 people, including Finance Ministers, attended the annual general meeting, ------- they discussed the world economy.
(A) where   (B) what   (C) whose   (D) which

**32.** It turned out that people living in New York City consume almost seven times ------- coffee as those living in other major cities in the U.S. do.
(A) much   (B) as much   (C) more   (D) much more

# Part 6

**Questions 33-36** refer to the following memo.

## The Newman's Annual Book Fair

Newman's Books is delighted to announce that its annual book fair will take place from the ------- week. We will prepare a special site for the fair which

    **33.** (A) soon
        (B) upcoming
        (C) extended
        (D) past

is crowded with many booklovers every year. Please visit the fourth floor of our building and enjoy shopping for your favorite book. As usual, all books and stationery with a red tag are offered at a 20 percent discount during the fair. We regret that you cannot get points on your loyalty card when you buy sale items.

This fair will ------- children's books and their authors from the United States and

    **34.** (A) feature
        (B) enclose
        (C) deal
        (D) forecast

around the world. We look forword to welcoming Camel Hamel, the renowned, award-winning author of *Naughty Cat*, a best-selling series of children's books, on the first day of the fair, December 13. Camel will hold a short reading from her latest book in the series, followed by a question-and-answer session. She will autograph her book for any audience member ------- buys her book.

                      **35.** (A) whose
                          (B) when
                          (C) which
                          (D) who

An advance reservation is not required but as seat availability is -------, please

                              **36.** (A) limiting
                                  (B) limitation
                                  (C) limited
                                  (D) limit

arrive early in order to secure good seats.

# Part 7

**Questions 37-40** refer to the following letters.

---

Dear Sir or Madam,

I am a frequent flyer on American Airways, but my flight from Tokyo to New York via Los Angeles was so terrible that I'm still completely disappointed.

My plane was supposed to arrive at JFK International Airport around 3 p.m. on Nov.28.

However, it took off from Haneda 2 hours late because of a mechanical problem and I missed my connecting flight. I finally reached my destination 5 hours after I was originally scheduled to arrive. I missed Thanksgiving dinner with my family.

On top of arriving late to my destination, I also had big problems with my baggage. I checked it in at Haneda International Airport and they promised that it would be checked through to JFK International Airport, my final destination. However, to my dismay, the baggage didn't arrive on the carousel. The gentleman at the lost baggage counter discovered that it had been left at L.A. International Airport. He explained that I had to collect and recheck my baggage on my point of entry to the U.S., but the woman at the American Airways check-in counter assured me that I didn't have to pick up my baggage at L.A. International Airport when I checked it in. I suspect she was not able to advise me properly due to her lack of knowledge or experience.

I expect quality services from you and request that you deal with this issue promptly. I look forward to hearing from you as soon as possible.

Sincerely,

*Jennifer Chandler*

---

Dear Miss Chandler,

Thank you for contacting us and letting us know about your recent experience with American Airways. Please accept our apologies for the inconveniences caused when your flight was delayed.

In addition, we're sorry your baggage was delayed. We understand the importance of ensuring that your baggage travels with you, and appreciate your feedback regarding our airport operations management to improve the quality of our passenger service agents.

As a token of our apology, we would like to offer you 3,000 miles. The miles will be credited to your account within 15 business days.

We look forward to a future opportunity to have you aboard.

Sincerely,

Jonathan Stewart
Managing Director
American Airways Customer Support Desk

37. When did Jennifer arrive at JFK International Airport?
    (A) Around 3 a.m. on Nov. 28.
    (B) Around 3 p.m. on Nov. 28.
    (C) Around 5 p.m. on Nov. 28.
    (D) Around 8 p.m. on Nov. 28.

38. Why didn't Jennifer pick up and recheck her baggage at L. A. International Airport?
    (A) Because she didn't have enough time at the airport.
    (B) Because the man at the lost baggage counter couldn't find it.
    (C) Because she thought it would be checked through to her final destination.
    (D) Because the woman at the check-in counter didn't check it.

39. What is the main purpose of Jonathan Stewart's letter?
    (A) To apologize to Jennifer
    (B) To make a complaint about American Airways' poor service
    (C) To suggest that Jennifer use her accumulated miles
    (D) To request Jennifer to contact American Airways' airport operations management

40. What will Jennifer get soon?
    (A) A new suitcase
    (B) 3,000 miles
    (C) Her account information
    (D) Flight schedules of American Airways

# Key Vocabulary

## Unit 1  Daily Life

### ●学校

1. commute — 動 通学する、通勤する
2. credit — 名 履修単位
3. graduate — 動 卒業する
4. major — 名 形 動 専攻(の、する)
5. master's degree [MA] — 名 修士号
6. registration, enrollment — 名 登録
7. scholarship — 名 奨学金
8. tuition — 名 授業料

### ●衣住

9. appliance — 名 電化製品、家電
10. ceiling — 名 天井
11. clothes — 名 衣服
    clothing — 名 衣類、衣料品
12. comfortable, cozy — 形 居心地の良い、快適な
13. condo(minium) — 名 分譲マンション
14. construction — 名 建設、建築工事
15. detergent — 名 洗剤
16. drawer — 名 引き出し
17. electricity — 名 電気
18. enter — 動 入る
    entrance — 名 入口
    exit — 名 出口
19. fabric — 名 生地
    textile — 名 織物
20. floor — 名 階、床
21. fold — 動 折りたたむ
22. furniture — 名 家具
23. hang — 動 吊るす
24. household — 名 形 世帯、家庭(の)
25. instrument — 名 器具
26. landlord — 名 家主
    tenant — 名 賃借人
27. laundry — 名 洗濯物、クリーニング店
    do the laundry — 動 洗濯する
    Laundromat — 名 コインランドリー
28. light fixture — 名 照明器具
29. monthly — 形 毎月の
    weekly — 形 毎週の
30. plumber — 名 配管工
31. property, real estate — 名 不動産
32. rent — 名 家賃
    — 動 賃貸する
33. repair, fix — 動 修理する
34. resident — 名 住人
35. stairs, staircase — 名 階段
    upstairs — 副 階上へ
    downstairs — 副 階下へ
36. suburb — 名 郊外
    urban — 形 都会の
37. turn on — 動 つける
    turn off — 動 消す
38. utilities — 名 公共料金

### ●その他

39. blackout — 名 停電
40. chores — 名 雑用
41. convenience — 名 便利さ
    inconvenience — 名 不便
42. emergency — 名 緊急事態
43. equip — 動 装備する
    equipment — 名 装備、設備
44. evacuate — 動 避難させる
45. grocery store — 名 食料雑貨店
46. humid — 形 湿気の多い
    humidity — 名 湿気
47. skyscraper — 名 超高層ビル
48. temperature — 名 温度、気温
    degrees — 名 度
49. warning — 名 警報、警告
50. weather forecast — 名 天気予報

# Unit 2  Eating Out & Leisure Activities

## ●外食

1. all-you-can-eat　名 形 食べ放題(の)
2. anniversary　名 記念日
3. appetite　名 食欲
4. atmosphere　名 雰囲気
5. attend　動 出席する
   attendance　名 出席
6. banquet　名 宴会
7. beverage　名 飲料
8. buffet　名 形 カウンター、立食(形式の)
9. cafeteria　名 セルフサービス式の食堂
10. casual　形 普段着の、気取らない
11. clerk　名 店員
12. complimentary, free　形 無料の
13. cuisine, dish, meal　名 料理
14. dessert　名 デザート
15. diner　名 食堂
16. farewell party　名 送別会
17. hold　動 開催する
18. ingredient　名 成分、原材料
19. order　名 動 注文(する)
20. participate in = take part in = join　動 参加する、加わる
21. prepare　動 準備する
22. quality　名 形 質、上質(な)
    quantity　名 量
23. reasonable　形 手頃な値段の
24. recipe　名 レシピ
25. register　名 レジ
    cashier　名 レジ係
26. serve　動 給仕する
27. taste　動 味がする
28. voucher　名 引換券
    coupon　名 割引券、クーポン

## ●娯楽

29. activity　名 活動
30. actor　名 俳優
    actress　名 女優
31. admission　名 入場、入会
32. appear　動 現れる、出演する
33. applaud　動 拍手する
    applause　名 拍手
34. attraction　名 魅力、客を引き付ける呼び物
35. award, prize　名 賞
36. box office　名 チケット売り場
37. critic　名 批評家、評論家
38. display　名 動 陳列(する)
39. donate　動 寄付する
    donation　名 寄付
40. excellent　形 優秀な、素晴らしい
41. exhibit　動 展示する、名 展示品
    exhibition　名 展覧会
42. favorite　名 形 お気に入り(の)
43. feature　動 目玉にする
44. impressive　形 印象的な
    impression　名 印象
45. matinee　名 昼興業、マチネー
46. performance　名 演奏、演技
47. reserve, book　動 予約する
    reservation, booking　名 予約
48. spectator, audience　名 観客、視聴者
49. stadium　名 スタジアム
50. theater　名 劇場

Key Vocabulary  109

# Unit 3  Cooking & Purchasing

## ●調理

- **1.** bake 動 焼く
  fry 動 揚げる
  grill 動 網焼きにする
  roast 動 炙る
- **2.** bread 名 パン
  bakery 名 パン屋
- **3.** boil 動 茹でる
  poach 動 さっと茹でる
  simmer 動 とろ火で煮る
- **4.** cupboard 名 食器棚
- **5.** cutlery 名 食卓用金物類
- **6.** dairy 名 形 乳製品(の)
- **7.** microwave oven 名 オーブンレンジ
  stove 名 コンロ
- **8.** pot 名 ポット
  kettle 名 やかん
  pan 名 平鍋
  fry pan 名 フライパン
- **9.** refrigerator, fridge 名 冷蔵庫
- **10.** sink 名 流し
- **11.** utensils 名 台所用品

## ●買い物

- **12.** bill 名 請求書、勘定書
- **13.** cash 名 現金
- **14.** change 名 おつり
- **15.** charge 名 手数料
  動 請求する
- **16.** clerk, staff 名 店員
- **17.** complaint 名 苦情、クレーム
- **18.** convenient 形 便利な
  inconvenient 形 不便な
- **19.** customer 名 顧客
  shopper 名 買い物客
- **20.** defect 名 欠陥
  defective product 名 欠陥品
- **21.** deliver 動 配達する
  delivery 名 配達
- **22.** discount 名 動 割引(く)
- **23.** dollar 名 ドル
- **24.** dozen 名 ダース[12個]
- **25.** estimate 名 見積り
  動 見積もる
- **26.** exchange, replace 動 交換する
- **27.** expensive 形 高価な
- **28.** for here or to go 句 こちらでお召し上がりですか、お持ち帰りですか
- **29.** fragile 形 壊れやすい、破損注意
- **30.** guarantee, warranty 名 保証
- **31.** inquire 動 尋ねる
  inquiry 名 質問、問合せ
- **32.** instructions 名 使用説明書
  specifications 名 仕様書
- **33.** invoice 名 送り状
- **34.** latest 形 名 最新の(もの)
- **35.** merchandise, goods, item 名 商品
- **36.** out of stock 句 在庫切れで
  in stock 句 入荷して
- **37.** package, parcel 名 小包
- **38.** pay 動 支払う
  payment 名 支払い
- **39.** purchase, buy 動 購入する
- **40.** questionnaire 名 アンケート用紙
  conduct a survey 句 アンケート調査を行う
- **41.** reasonable 形 手頃な値段の
  inexpensive 形 割安の
  cheap 形 安っぽい
- **42.** receipt 名 レシート
- **43.** refund 名 動 返金(する)
- **44.** return, take back 動 返品する
- **45.** shipping and handling cost 名 発送手数料
- **46.** subscribe to 動 ～を定期購入・購読する
  subscription 名 定期購入・購読
- **47.** suit(+人) 動 ～に似合う
- **48.** toll-free 形 副 フリーダイアルの(で)
- **49.** up to 句 最大～まで
- **50.** vending machine 名 自動販売機

# Unit 4  Traffic & Travel

## ●交通

1. area 名 地域
   region 名 区域
2. available 形 入手できる、利用できる
3. commute 動 通勤する
4. crosswalk 名 横断歩道
   intersection 名 交差点
5. expressway 名 高速道路
   highway 名 幹線道路
6. fare 名 運賃、料金
7. get on 動 乗る
   get off 動 降りる
8. metropolitan 形 大都市の
   downtown 形 繁華街の
9. parking lot 名 駐車場
10. sidewalk, walkway 名 歩道
11. pedestrian 名 歩行者
12. proceed, head 動 進む、向かう
13. traffic jam 名 交通渋滞
14. transportation 名 輸送機関、乗物
15. vehicle 名 乗物、車

## ●旅行

16. accommodate 動 収容できる
    accommodation 名 宿泊(設備)
17. aisle-seat 名 通路側の席
    window-seat 名 窓側の席
18. arrival 名 到着
    departure 名 出発
19. baggage, luggage 名 手荷物
20. baggage claim (area) 名 手荷物受取所
21. belongings 名 所持品
    valuables 名 貴重品
22. board 動 乗り込む
23. book, reserve 動 予約する
    booking, reservation 名 予約
24. bound for 形 ～行きの
25. cancel 動 中止する
    = call off
    postpone 動 延期する
    = put off
26. check in 名動 チェックイン(する)
    check out 名動 チェックアウト(する)
27. confirm 動 確認する
28. connect 動 ～に接続する・連絡する
    connection 名 接続、連絡
29. customs 名 税関、関税
30. declare 動 申告する
31. delay 名動 遅延(させる)
32. destination 名 目的地
33. domestic flight 名 国内線
    international flight 名 国際線
34. fasten 動 締める、固定する
35. flight attendant, cabin attendant 名 客室乗務員
36. itinerary 名 旅程表
37. landmark 名 目印(となるもの)
38. local 形 現地の、地元の
39. lost and found 名 遺失物取扱所
40. one-way ticket 名 片道切符
    round-trip ticket 名 往復切符
41. package tour 名 パック旅行
42. passenger 名 乗客
43. sightseeing 名 観光
44. souvenir 名 記念品、土産
45. take off 動 離陸する
    land 動 着陸する
46. terminal 名 終点、始点
47. time table 名 時刻表
48. travel agency 名 旅行代理店
49. vacant 形 空いている
    vacancy 名 空室、空席
50. via, by way of 前 ～経由で

# Unit 5 Advertising & ICT

## ●広告

- □ 1. advertise　動 広告する、宣伝する
  advertisement　名 広告
- □ 2. affordable　形 購入できる、手頃な
- □ 3. announce　動 公表する、発表する
  announcement　名 公表、発表
- □ 4. article　名 記事
- □ 5. attractive　形 魅力的な
- □ 6. broadcast, air　名 動 放送(する)
- □ 7. brochure　名 パンフレット
- □ 8. bulletin　名 掲示、速報
- □ 9. commerce　名 商業
- □ 10. commercial　形 商業の　名 コマーシャル
- □ 11. consume　動 消費する
- □ 12. copyright　名 著作権
- □ 13. flyer, leaflet　名 チラシ
- □ 14. headline　名 見出し、表題
- □ 15. impressive　形 印象的な
- □ 16. influence　名 動 影響(を及ぼす)
- □ 17. issue　名 動 発行(する)
- □ 18. launch, release　名 動 発売(する)、開始(する)
- □ 19. marketing　名 マーケティング
- □ 20. outstanding　形 目立つ、優れた
- □ 21. promotion campaign　名 販促キャンペーン
- □ 22. public relations　名 広報活動、PR
- □ 23. publish　動 出版する
  publisher　名 出版社
- □ 24. recommend　動 推薦する、勧める
- □ 25. spokesperson　名 広報担当者
- □ 26. stress　動 強調する
- □ 27. various　形 さまざまな

## ●情報通信技術

- □ 28. access　名 アクセス　動 接続する
- □ 29. browse　動 閲覧する、検索する
  browser　名 ブラウザ[閲覧ソフト]
- □ 30. cellphone, mobile phone　名 携帯電話
  smart phone　名 スマートフォン
- □ 31. customize　動 自分好みに変更する
- □ 32. delete　名 動 削除(する)
- □ 33. e-commerce　名 電子商取引
- □ 34. enter　動 入力する
- □ 35. function　名 機能
- □ 36. gadget　名 小型デジタル機器
- □ 37. information security　名 情報セキュリティ
- □ 38. install　動 インストールする
- □ 39. laptop　名 形 ノートパソコン(の)
- □ 40. manual　名 手引書、説明書
- □ 41. online　形 オンラインの
- □ 42. patch　名 プログラムの修正
- □ 43. recognition　名 認識
- □ 44. reply　名 動 返信(する)
- □ 45. save　動 保存する
- □ 46. sign up　動 サインアップ[加入]する
- □ 47. software　名 ソフトウェア
  hardware　名 ハードウェア
- □ 48. spams　名 迷惑メール
  virus　名 ウィルス
- □ 49. update　名 動 アップデート(する)、更新(する)
- □ 50. up-to-date, cutting-edge, state-of-the-art　形 最新式の、最先端の

# Unit 6  Production & Logistics

## ●製造

1. adjust　動 調整する
2. architect　名 建築家、設計者
   architecture　名 建築
3. artificial　形 人工的な
   synthetic　形 合成の
4. assembly line　名 組み立てライン
5. capacity　名 生産能力
6. caution　名 注意
7. chemical　名形 化学薬品(の)
8. construction site　名 建設現場
9. develop　動 開発する
   development　名 開発
10. dispose　動 処理する
    disposal　名 処理
11. durable　形 耐性のある
12. engineering　名 工学(技術)
13. experiment　名動 実験(する)
14. facility　名 設備、施設
    plant, factory　名 工場
15. garage　名 車庫、修理整備工場
16. gas station　名 ガソリンスタンド
17. hazard　名 危険
    hazardous　形 危険な
18. industrial waste　名 産業ごみ
19. innovate　動 革新する
20. inspect　動 検査する、点検する
    inspection　名 検査、点検
21. laboratory　名 実験室、研究室
22. machinery　名 機械装置
23. maintenance　名 整備、メンテ
24. manufacture　名動 製造(する)
    manufacturer　名 製造業者、メーカー
25. material　名 材料、原料
26. natural resources　名 天然資源
27. operation　名 操作、運転
28. patent　名形 特許(の)
29. product　名 製品
    production　名 生産
    productivity　名 生産性
30. prototype　名 試作品
31. renovate　動 改築する
32. renew　動 一新する
    remodel　動 改造する
33. technology　名 科学技術

## ●物流

34. cargo　名 積荷、貨物
    freight　名 貨物運送
35. container　名 貨物用コンテナ
36. distribution　名 流通
37. dock　名 埠頭
    harbor　名 港
38. import　名動 輸入(する)
    export　名動 輸出(する)
39. increase 名動 増加(する、させる)
    decrease, reduce 名動 減少(する、させる)
40. load　名 積荷
    動 積み込む
41. logistics　名 物流
42. pack　名 荷物
    動 梱包する
43. pile, stack　動 積み上げる
44. prompt　形 迅速な
    promptly　副 迅速に
45. provide　動 供給する
46. retailer　名 小売業者
    wholesaler　名 卸売業者
47. ship　動 輸送する、発送する
    shipment　名 輸送、発送
48. stock, inventory　名 在庫
49. supplier　名 供給業者
    carrier　名 配達員
50. warehouse, storage　名 倉庫

# Unit 7  Business & Economics

1. additional fee, extra charge 名 追加手数料、追加料金
2. advantage 名 有利な点、強み
3. agenda 名 議題
4. accept 動 受け入れる、受諾する
   agree 動 同意する
5. analyze 動 分析する
   analysis 名 分析
6. annual convention 名 年次総会
7. boost 動 伸ばす、増やす
8. budget 名 予算(案)
9. collaborate 動 共同研究する
   collaboration 名 共同研究
10. competitive 形 競争力のある
    competitor 名 競争相手
11. compromise 名 動 妥協(する)
12. confident 形 自信のある
13. consult 動 相談する
14. consume 動 消費する
    consumer 名 消費者
    consumption 名 消費
15. contract 名 動 契約(する)
16. client 名 顧客、取引先
17. damage 名 動 損害(を与える)
18. deal 名 取引、契約
    動 取り扱う
19. decade 名 10年間
20. decline 動 衰退する
    deteriorate 動 悪化する
21. demand 名 需要
    動 要求する
    supply 名 動 供給(する)
22. depression 名 長期的不景気
    recession 名 一時的景気後退
23. effect 名 効果
    effective 形 効果的な
24. exchange rate 名 為替相場
25. expand, enlarge 動 拡大する
    downsize 動 縮小する
26. firm, company, corporation, enterprise 名 会社、企業
27. found, establish 動 設立する
28. bankruptcy 名 倒産、破産
    go bankrupt 動 倒産する、破産する
29. institution 名 制度、機関
30. investigate 動 調査する、研究する
31. launch 動 開始する、発売する
32. merger, M & A [merger and acquisition] 名 合併吸収
33. negotiate 動 交渉する
    negotiation 名 交渉
34. potential customer 名 潜在的な客
    prospective customer 名 見込み客
35. profit 名 利益
    loss 名 損失
    profitable 形 儲かる
36. proposal, suggestion 名 提案
37. prosperous 形 繁盛している
38. regulation 名 規制
    deregulation 名 規制緩和
39. second quarter 名 第2四半期
40. sign 動 署名する
    signature 名 署名、調印
41. skyrocket, soar 動 急上昇する
42. stimulate 動 刺激する
43. stock market 名 株式市場
44. stockholder, shareholder 名 株主
45. strategy 名 戦略
46. target 名 対象、達成目標
    形 販売対象にする
47. trade 名 動 貿易(する)、取引(する)
48. transfer 名 動 移転(させる)、異動(する)
49. unemployment rate 名 失業率
50. venture 名 投機的事業

# Unit 8  Employment & Personnel

●雇用

1. MBA [Master of Business Administration]　名 経営修士(号)
2. academic background　名 学歴
3. apply for　動 〜に申し込む
   applicant　名 応募者
   application form　名 応募用紙
4. appreciate　動 感謝する
5. career　名 経歴
6. classified ads　名 求人・求職広告
7. current, present　形 現在の
8. decline　動 丁寧に断る
9. employ, hire　動 雇用する
   employment, hiring　名 雇用、採用
10. employee　名 従業員
    employer　名 雇い主
11. experience　名 動 経験(する)
    experienced　形 経験豊富な
12. fill out/in　動 記入する
13. full-time　形 常勤の
    part-time, temporary　形 非常勤の
14. interview　名 動 面接(する)
15. job opening, vacancy　名 空きポスト、欠員
16. occupation　名 職業、職
17. opportunity　名 機会
18. qualification　名 資格
    certificate　名 証明書
19. recommend　動 推薦する
    recommendation　名 推薦(状)
20. recruit　動 人員を募集する
    名 新入社員
21. résumé, CV [curriculum vitae]　名 履歴書
22. salary, wage　名 給料、賃金
23. train　動 訓練する、教育する

●人事

24. CEO [chief executive officer]　名 最高経営責任者
25. board of directors　名 取締役会、理事会
26. branch　名 支社、支店
    headquarters, head office　名 本社、本店
27. candidate　名 候補者
28. chair(person)　名 議長
29. competent, efficient　形 有能な
30. contribute　動 貢献する
    contribution　名 貢献
31. designate　動 指名する
    appoint, assign　動 任命する
32. diligent, industrious　形 勤勉な
33. evaluate　動 評価する
    evaluation　名 評価
34. fire, dismiss　動 解雇する
    layoff　名 一時的解雇
35. HR [human resources], personnel　名 人事
36. income　名 収入
37. manager　名 部長
    executive　名 形 管理職(の)
38. performance　名 業績
39. previous, former　形 前の
40. promising　形 前途有望な
41. promote　動 昇進させる
    promotion　名 昇進
42. proper, appropriate, suitable　形 適切な
43. R & D [research and development]　名 研究開発
44. replace　動 〜の後任になる
45. resign, quit　動 辞職する、辞任する
46. retire　動 定年退職する
47. department, division　名 部(門)
    section　名 課
48. subsidiary　名 系列子会社
49. transfer　名 動 転勤(する)、異動(する)、移転(させる)
50. vice-president　名 副社長

Key Vocabulary ○ 115

# Unit 9  Office Work & Correspondence

● 社内業務

- [ ] 1. adopt 　　　　　　動 採用する、導入する
- [ ] 2. apologize 　　　　動 謝罪する
       apology 　　　　　名 謝罪
- [ ] 3. approximately 　副 およそ、約
- [ ] 4. arrange 　　　　　動 手配する
- [ ] 5. attend a meeting 　動 会議に出席する
- [ ] 6. be responsible for 　句 〜に責任がある
       be in charge of 　句 〜を担当して
- [ ] 7. boss, supervisor 　名 上司
       subordinate 　名 部下
- [ ] 8. calculate 　　　　動 計算する
       calculation 　　名 計算
- [ ] 9. clerk 　　　　　　名 事務員、店員
- [ ] 10. colleague, coworker 　名 同僚
- [ ] 11. committee 　　　名 委員会
- [ ] 12. complaint 　　　名 不満、苦情、クレーム
- [ ] 13. conclude 　　　　動 結論付ける
        conclusion 　　名 結論
- [ ] 14. conference 　　名 会議、協議会
- [ ] 15. confirm 　　　　動 確かめる
        confirmation 　名 確認
- [ ] 16. deadline 　　　　名 締め切り
- [ ] 17. deal with, handle 　動 処理する
- [ ] 18. document 　　　名 文書
- [ ] 19. draft 　　　　　　名 原稿、草稿
- [ ] 20. encourage A to do 　句 Aに〜するよう促す
- [ ] 21. equipment 　　　名 備品
- [ ] 22. flexible 　　　　形 柔軟な、融通のきく
- [ ] 23. hand in, submit 　動 提出する
- [ ] 24. handout 　　　　名 配布資料、プリント
- [ ] 25. identification 　名 身分証明書
- [ ] 26. incentive 　　　名 報奨(金)
        　　　　　　　　形 やる気を起こさせる
- [ ] 27. invoice 　　　　名 送り状
- [ ] 28. management 　名 管理、経営
- [ ] 29. notify, inform 　動 知らせる
        notification 　名 通知
- [ ] 30. photocopier, copier 　名 コピー機
- [ ] 31. presentation 　名 プレゼン
- [ ] 32. receptionist 　名 受付係
        secretary 　　名 秘書
- [ ] 33. routine 　　　　名 決まりきった仕事
- [ ] 34. sales quota 　名 売上ノルマ
- [ ] 35. sales representative 　名 営業担当者
- [ ] 36. seminar 　　　　名 講習会
        workshop 　　名 研修会
- [ ] 37. solution 　　　　名 解決(策)
- [ ] 38. staple 　　　　　動 ホッチキスで留める
        stapler 　　　　名 ホッチキス
- [ ] 39. stationery 　　　名 文房具
        office supplies 　名 事務用品
- [ ] 40. work overtime 　動 残業する

● 通信

- [ ] 41. attach 　　　　　動 添付する
- [ ] 42. by express 　　句 速達で
- [ ] 43. confidential 　　形 秘密の、親展
- [ ] 44. enclose 　　　　動 同封する
- [ ] 45. envelope 　　　名 封筒
        stamp 　　　　名 切手
- [ ] 46. forward 　　　　動 転送する
- [ ] 47. leave a message 　動 伝言を残す
        take a message 　動 伝言を受ける
- [ ] 48. on another line 　句 他の電話に出ていて
- [ ] 49. postage 　　　　名 郵便料金
- [ ] 50. receive 　　　　動 受け取る

# Unit 10  Health & the Environment

## ●健康

- 1. ambulance　名 救急車
- 2. benefit, allowance　名 手当、給付
- 3. cancer　名 癌
- 4. checkup　名 健康診断
- 5. cough　名 咳
  fever　名 熱
- 6. cover　動 保障する
  coverage　名 保障(額)
- 7. cure, treatment　名 治療
- 8. day care　名 託児所
- 9. dentist　名 歯科医
- 10. disease, illness　名 病気
- 11. fatal　形 致命的な
  serious　形 重症の
- 12. flu　名 インフルエンザ
  cold　名 風邪
- 13. health insurance　名 健康保険
- 14. headache　名 頭痛
  toothache　名 歯痛
- 15. sick leave　名 病気休暇
  paid leave/vacation　名 有給休暇
- 16. medicine, drug　名 内服薬
- 17. obesity　名 肥満
  obese　形 肥満の
  overweight　名 形 肥満(の)
- 18. patient　名 患者
  　　形 忍耐強い
- 19. pension　名 年金
- 20. pharmacy　名 薬局
  pharmaceutical　形 製薬の
- 21. physician　名 内科医
  surgeon　名 外科医
- 22. prescribe　動 処方する
  prescription　名 処方箋
- 23. prevent　動 予防する
- 24. recover　動 回復する
  recovery　名 回復
- 25. side effect　名 副作用
- 26. social security　名 社会保障(制度)
- 27. suffer from　句 〜を患う
  ＝ come down with
- 28. surgery, operation　名 手術
- 29. symptom　名 症状
- 30. take care of　句 世話をする
  ＝ look after
- 31. urgent　形 緊急の
  emergency　名 救急
- 32. welfare　名 福利厚生、福祉
- 33. X-rays　名 レントゲン写真

## ●環境

- 34. acid rain　名 酸性雨
- 35. alternative source of energy　名 代替エネルギー源
- 36. atmosphere　名 大気、空気
- 37. carbon dioxide　名 二酸化炭素
- 38. eco-friendly, sustainable　形 環境に優しい
- 39. eliminate, remove　動 除去する
- 40. emit　動 排出する
  emission　名 排出
- 41. environment　名 環境
- 42. garbage, waste, trash　名 ごみ
- 43. greenhouse effect　名 温室効果
- 44. global warming　名 地球温暖化
- 45. pollution　名 汚染、公害
- 46. predict, anticipate　動 予想する
- 47. protect　動 保護する
- 48. recycle　動 再利用する
  recycling　名 再利用
  reusable　形 再利用可能な
- 49. tend　動 傾向がある
  tendency　名 傾向
- 50. toxic　形 有毒な

# Unit 11　Finance & Banking

- 1. ATM [automatic teller machine]　名 現金自動支払機
- 2. PIN [personal identification number]　名 暗証番号
- 3. accept　動 受け入れる
- 4. account　名 銀行口座
- 5. accountant　名 会計士、会計係
- 6. annual　形 年一回の
- 7. asset　名 資産
- 8. balance sheet　名 貸借対照表
- 9. bank clerk, teller　名 銀行員
- 10. bankruptcy　名 破産、倒産
- 11. bottom line　名 最終損益
- 12. business days　名 営業日
     business hours　名 営業時間
- 13. capital　名 資本(金)
- 14. check　名 小切手
- 15. check the balance　動 預金残高を調べる
- 16. close the book　動 決算する
- 17. consultant　名 顧問、コンサルタント
- 18. cost, expense, expenditure　名 経費、費用
- 19. currency　名 通貨
- 20. debt, liabilities　名 負債、債務
- 21. deposit　動 預金する
     withdraw　動 引き出す
- 22. due　形 支払期日の来た、満期の
     overdue　形 期限が過ぎた、滞納の
- 23. exhaust　動 使い果たす
- 24. expect, anticipate　動 予想する
- 25. expire　動 期限が切れて無効となる
- 26. explain, describe　動 説明する
     = account for
- 27. figure　名 数字、図
- 28. finance　名 財政、金融　動 融資する
     financial　形 財務の、金融の
- 29. fiscal year [FY]　名 事業年度
- 30. fund　名 基金　動 資金提供する
- 31. get into the red　動 赤字になる
     get into the black　動 黒字になる
     in the red　形 赤字で
     in the black　形 黒字で
- 32. gross profit　名 売上総利益
     net profit　名 純利益
- 33. in advance, beforehand　副 前もって
- 34. interest　名 利子、利息
- 35. invest　動 投資する
     investment　名 投資
- 36. loan　名 貸付　動 貸す
- 37. outstanding　名形 未払い(の)
- 38. procedure　名 手続き
- 39. propose　動 提案する
- 40. prospect　名 見通し
- 41. reliable　形 信頼できる
- 42. reminder　名 督促状
- 43. require　動 要求する
     = call for
- 44. revenue　名 収益、収入、歳入
- 45. save　動 貯金する
     savings　名 貯蓄
- 46. short-term　形 短期の
     long-term　形 長期の
- 47. stock exchange　名 証券取引所
- 48. tax　名 税金
- 49. transfer　動 振り込む
     remit　動 送金する
- 50. valid　形 有効な

# Unit 12 Law & Administration

## ●司法

1. abolish 動 廃止する
   = do away with
2. allow, permit 動 許可する
   ban, prohibit 動 禁止する
3. arrest 名動 逮捕(する)
4. attorney, lawyer 名 弁護士
5. clue 名 手がかり、糸口
6. commit a crime 動 犯罪を犯す
7. compensate 動 賠償する
   compensation 名 賠償
8. confess 動 白状する
   confession 名 告白、白状
9. detective 名 刑事
   agent 名 捜査官
   police officer 名 警察官
10. evidence 名 証拠
11. fine 名 罰金
12. file a law suit, sue 動 告訴する
13. fraud 名 詐欺(師)
14. guilty 形 有罪の
    innocent 形 無罪の
15. inherit 動 相続する
    inheritance 名 相続(権)
16. impose 動 課す
17. insist, assert 動 主張する
18. investigate 動 捜査する、取り調べる
    investigation 名 捜査
19. judge 名 裁判官、判事
    jury 名 陪審員団
20. judgment 名 裁判官の判決
    verdict 名 陪審員の評決
21. legal 形 合法の
    illegal 形 違法の
22. mention, state 動 述べる
23. neglect 名 無視、怠慢
    動 無視する、怠る
24. plaintiff 名 原告
    defendant 名 被告
25. observe 動 遵守する
26. prosecutor 名 検事
27. punish 動 罰する
    punishment 名 罰
28. Supreme Court 名 最高裁判所
29. suspect 名 容疑者
    criminal 名 犯罪者
30. victim 名 被害者
31. witness 名 目撃者
    動 目撃する

## ●行政

32. authorities 名 当局
    officials 名 当局者、職員
33. city council 名 市議会
34. city hall 名 市役所
35. conservative 形 保守的な
    radical 形 急進的な
36. county 名 郡
    state 名 (アメリカの)州
37. cover 動 報道する
    coverage 名 報道
38. democracy 名 民主主義
39. elect 動 選出する
    election 名 選挙
    vote 名動 投票(する)
40. friction 名 摩擦
    conflict 名 対立
41. government 名 政府
42. legislation 名 立法
43. mayor 名 市長
    governor 名 知事
44. ministry 名 省
45. municipal 形 地方自治の
46. policy, measure 名 政策
47. political party 名 政党
48. press conference 名 記者会見
49. senator 名 上院議員
    representative 名 下院議員
50. support 動 ～に賛成する
    = be for, = be in favor of
    object to 動 反対する
    = be against
    refuse, reject 動 拒否する
    = turn down

Key Vocabulary 119

◀ここからはがしてください

このシールをはがすと
CheckLink 利用のための
「教科書固有番号」が
記載されています。

一度はがすと元に戻すことは
できませんのでご注意下さい。

4004 Seize the Core of
the TOEIC Test　CheckLink

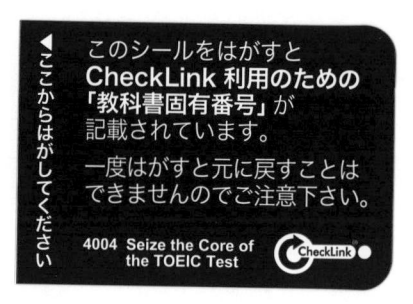

本書には CD（別売）があります

## SEIZE THE CORE OF THE TOEIC® TEST
TOEIC®テスト コアをつかんで完全攻略

2015 年 1 月 20 日 初版第 1 刷発行
2024 年 4 月 10 日 初版第 10 刷発行

著　者　　安　丸　雅　子
　　　　　砂　川　典　子
　　　　　秋　好　礼　子
　　　　　十　時　　　康
　　　　　渡　邉　晶　子
　　　　　Andrew Zitzmann

発行者　　福　岡　正　人
発行所　　株式会社　金　星　堂

（〒101-0051）東京都千代田区神田神保町 3-21
　　　　　Tel. (03) 3263-3828 (営業部)
　　　　　　　 (03) 3263-3997 (編集部)
　　　　　Fax (03) 3263-0716
　　　　　http://www.kinsei-do.co.jp

編集担当　松本明子　　　　　　　　　Printed in Japan
印刷所・製本所／三美印刷株式会社
本書の無断複製・複写は著作権法上での例外を除き禁じられています。
本書を代行業者等の第三者に依頼してスキャンやデジタル化することは、
たとえ個人や家庭内での利用であっても認められておりません。
落丁・乱丁本はお取り替えいたします。

ISBN978-4-7647-4004-4　C1082

# Review Test 1 マークシート

| 学籍番号 |
|---|
| ふりがな |
| 名前 |

## LISTENING SECTION

### Part 1

| No. | ANSWER |
|---|---|
| | A B C D |
| 1 | Ⓐ Ⓑ Ⓒ Ⓓ |
| 2 | Ⓐ Ⓑ Ⓒ Ⓓ |
| 3 | Ⓐ Ⓑ Ⓒ Ⓓ |
| 4 | Ⓐ Ⓑ Ⓒ Ⓓ |

### Part 2

| No. | ANSWER |
|---|---|
| | A B C |
| 5 | Ⓐ Ⓑ Ⓒ |
| 6 | Ⓐ Ⓑ Ⓒ |
| 7 | Ⓐ Ⓑ Ⓒ |
| 8 | Ⓐ Ⓑ Ⓒ |
| 9 | Ⓐ Ⓑ Ⓒ |
| 10 | Ⓐ Ⓑ Ⓒ |

### Part 3

| No. | ANSWER |
|---|---|
| | A B C D |
| 11 | Ⓐ Ⓑ Ⓒ Ⓓ |
| 12 | Ⓐ Ⓑ Ⓒ Ⓓ |
| 13 | Ⓐ Ⓑ Ⓒ Ⓓ |
| 14 | Ⓐ Ⓑ Ⓒ Ⓓ |
| 15 | Ⓐ Ⓑ Ⓒ Ⓓ |
| 16 | Ⓐ Ⓑ Ⓒ Ⓓ |

### Part 4

| No. | ANSWER |
|---|---|
| | A B C D |
| 17 | Ⓐ Ⓑ Ⓒ Ⓓ |
| 18 | Ⓐ Ⓑ Ⓒ Ⓓ |
| 19 | Ⓐ Ⓑ Ⓒ Ⓓ |
| 20 | Ⓐ Ⓑ Ⓒ Ⓓ |
| 21 | Ⓐ Ⓑ Ⓒ Ⓓ |
| 22 | Ⓐ Ⓑ Ⓒ Ⓓ |

## READING SECTION

### Part 5

| No. | ANSWER |
|---|---|
| | A B C D |
| 23 | Ⓐ Ⓑ Ⓒ Ⓓ |
| 24 | Ⓐ Ⓑ Ⓒ Ⓓ |
| 25 | Ⓐ Ⓑ Ⓒ Ⓓ |
| 26 | Ⓐ Ⓑ Ⓒ Ⓓ |
| 27 | Ⓐ Ⓑ Ⓒ Ⓓ |
| 28 | Ⓐ Ⓑ Ⓒ Ⓓ |
| 29 | Ⓐ Ⓑ Ⓒ Ⓓ |
| 30 | Ⓐ Ⓑ Ⓒ Ⓓ |
| 31 | Ⓐ Ⓑ Ⓒ Ⓓ |
| 32 | Ⓐ Ⓑ Ⓒ Ⓓ |

### Part 6

| No. | ANSWER |
|---|---|
| | A B C D |
| 33 | Ⓐ Ⓑ Ⓒ Ⓓ |
| 34 | Ⓐ Ⓑ Ⓒ Ⓓ |
| 35 | Ⓐ Ⓑ Ⓒ Ⓓ |
| 36 | Ⓐ Ⓑ Ⓒ Ⓓ |

### Part 7

| No. | ANSWER |
|---|---|
| | A B C D |
| 37 | Ⓐ Ⓑ Ⓒ Ⓓ |
| 38 | Ⓐ Ⓑ Ⓒ Ⓓ |
| 39 | Ⓐ Ⓑ Ⓒ Ⓓ |
| 40 | Ⓐ Ⓑ Ⓒ Ⓓ |

# Review Test 2 マークシート

学籍番号

ふりがな

名　前

## LISTENING SECTION

### Part 1

| No. | ANSWER<br>A B C D |
|---|---|
| 1 | Ⓐ Ⓑ Ⓒ Ⓓ |
| 2 | Ⓐ Ⓑ Ⓒ Ⓓ |
| 3 | Ⓐ Ⓑ Ⓒ Ⓓ |
| 4 | Ⓐ Ⓑ Ⓒ Ⓓ |

### Part 2

| No. | ANSWER<br>A B C |
|---|---|
| 5 | Ⓐ Ⓑ Ⓒ |
| 6 | Ⓐ Ⓑ Ⓒ |
| 7 | Ⓐ Ⓑ Ⓒ |
| 8 | Ⓐ Ⓑ Ⓒ |
| 9 | Ⓐ Ⓑ Ⓒ |
| 10 | Ⓐ Ⓑ Ⓒ |

### Part 3

| No. | ANSWER<br>A B C D |
|---|---|
| 11 | Ⓐ Ⓑ Ⓒ Ⓓ |
| 12 | Ⓐ Ⓑ Ⓒ Ⓓ |
| 13 | Ⓐ Ⓑ Ⓒ Ⓓ |
| 14 | Ⓐ Ⓑ Ⓒ Ⓓ |
| 15 | Ⓐ Ⓑ Ⓒ Ⓓ |
| 16 | Ⓐ Ⓑ Ⓒ Ⓓ |

### Part 4

| No. | ANSWER<br>A B C D |
|---|---|
| 17 | Ⓐ Ⓑ Ⓒ Ⓓ |
| 18 | Ⓐ Ⓑ Ⓒ Ⓓ |
| 19 | Ⓐ Ⓑ Ⓒ Ⓓ |
| 20 | Ⓐ Ⓑ Ⓒ Ⓓ |
| 21 | Ⓐ Ⓑ Ⓒ Ⓓ |
| 22 | Ⓐ Ⓑ Ⓒ Ⓓ |

## READING SECTION

### Part 5

| No. | ANSWER<br>A B C D |
|---|---|
| 23 | Ⓐ Ⓑ Ⓒ Ⓓ |
| 24 | Ⓐ Ⓑ Ⓒ Ⓓ |
| 25 | Ⓐ Ⓑ Ⓒ Ⓓ |
| 26 | Ⓐ Ⓑ Ⓒ Ⓓ |
| 27 | Ⓐ Ⓑ Ⓒ Ⓓ |
| 28 | Ⓐ Ⓑ Ⓒ Ⓓ |
| 29 | Ⓐ Ⓑ Ⓒ Ⓓ |
| 30 | Ⓐ Ⓑ Ⓒ Ⓓ |

### Part 6

| No. | ANSWER<br>A B C D |
|---|---|
| 31 | Ⓐ Ⓑ Ⓒ Ⓓ |
| 32 | Ⓐ Ⓑ Ⓒ Ⓓ |
| 33 | Ⓐ Ⓑ Ⓒ Ⓓ |
| 34 | Ⓐ Ⓑ Ⓒ Ⓓ |
| 35 | Ⓐ Ⓑ Ⓒ Ⓓ |
| 36 | Ⓐ Ⓑ Ⓒ Ⓓ |

### Part 7

| No. | ANSWER<br>A B C D |
|---|---|
| 37 | Ⓐ Ⓑ Ⓒ Ⓓ |
| 38 | Ⓐ Ⓑ Ⓒ Ⓓ |
| 39 | Ⓐ Ⓑ Ⓒ Ⓓ |
| 40 | Ⓐ Ⓑ Ⓒ Ⓓ |